I0025030

'Despite our personal, interpersonal, and professional lives constantly being shaped by our values and belief systems, the common discourse on spirituality is often reduced to religion, with little exploration of its intricate dimensionalities and complexities. This practice manual provides an honest, informed, and in-depth discussion of the various constitutions of spirituality, while examining its intersection with religion for informing professional practice in the human services. It is long overdue and highly commendable, a refreshing, important and comprehensive addition to the literature; a volume that makes us think, reflect, and act upon our true north with conviction and determination.'

Dr Andy Hau Yan Ho, *Provost's Chair Professor in Psychology, Nanyang Technological University, Singapore*

'This is not a textbook in the typical sense and use of the term "manual" should not suggest a functional "how to" manual. The authors draw on their considerable expertise to challenge thinking, promote reflection, and improve practice through a framework that takes complex concepts and makes them manageable and accessible. The values and knowledge of the authors shine through and suggest the integration of theory, practice, and values by promoting a "theorizing practice" approach. Importantly, the manual makes a compelling case for the importance of understanding people's spiritual needs as that which enables people to "give expression to their worldview". This thought-provoking approach is helpful, and the use of "Reflective moments" encourages reflection and understanding. The exercises at the end of each chapter require the reader to think and to apply that thinking to complex situations, thereby better understanding how our own values inform what we do and how we practise.'

Gerry Rice, *Dean for Students, University of the West of England*

'This is a welcome second edition of the *Spirituality and Religious* practice manual by Neil Thompson and the late Bernard Moss. The authors identified an important area of professional practice, revealing an underdeveloped curriculum area, relating to spirituality and religion and have updated the manual to further explore and update the topic in the context of changing societal and contemporary challenges. They do not expect the manual to do justice to all religious or spiritual denominations, nor address the complexities of people-based practice across all faith, spiritual, religious, and cultural contexts. Rather, they use a social justice and human rights perspective to consider religious and spiritual diversity by consideration of the practice context, using anti-oppressive principles. The manual provides a framework for students, practitioners, managers and academics to critically explore these topics, and it provides a reflective resource to interrogate knowledge and understanding in this critical domain.'

Dr Paula McFadden, *Professor of Social Work, Ulster University*

Spirituality and Religion in Human Services

Spirituality, whether or not rooted in religion, is a core feature of what it means to be human. This important practice manual explains why spirituality and religion should be a fundamental consideration for professions that are centred around helping people tackle their problems and fulfil their potential.

The authors draw on their considerable expertise to challenge thinking, promote reflection and improve practice through a framework that takes complex concepts and makes them manageable and accessible. By fusing together theory, practice and values, a theorizing practice approach is promoted to encourage reflection and understanding, with exercises at the end of each chapter to stimulate the reader to think about how values inform practice.

This insightful guide equips a wide range of practitioners and managers with an understanding of spirituality and religion within day-to-day practice to support others and nurture best results.

Neil Thompson is a well-known and highly respected author in social work and the human relations field more broadly. He is currently a visiting professor at The Open University and Wrexham University. His online platform, The Neil Thompson Academy, offers a range of learning opportunities, including leadership qualifications.

Bernard Moss was Emeritus Professor of Social Work Education and Spirituality at Staffordshire University, where he began working with social work students in 1993. His particular teaching interests focused on communication skills, studies in death, dying and bereavement, and mediation studies.

Practice Manuals for Busy Professionals

Managing Stress, 2ⁿᵈ edition
Neil Thompson

Effective Problem Solving, 2ⁿᵈ edition
Neil Thompson

Crisis Intervention, 3ʳᵈ edition
Neil Thompson

Care of Older People: A Values Perspective, 2ⁿᵈ edition
Sue Thompson

Spirituality and Religion in Human Services: A Guide for Practitioners and Managers, 2ⁿᵈ edition
Neil Thompson and Bernard Moss

Anti-Racist Practice, 2ⁿᵈ edition
Neil Thompson

Values-Based Practice: A Guide for Practitioners and Managers, 2ⁿᵈ edition
Neil Thompson and Bernard Moss

Spirituality and Religion in Human Services

A Guide for Practitioners and Managers

Second Edition

Neil Thompson and Bernard Moss

With a Foreword by Professor Margaret Holloway

Routledge
Taylor & Francis Group

LONDON AND NEW YORK

Designed cover image: Getty Images

Second edition published 2026
by Routledge
4 Park Square, Milton Park, Abingdon, Oxon, OX14 4RN

and by Routledge
605 Third Avenue, New York, NY 10158

Routledge is an imprint of the Taylor & Francis Group, an informa business

© 2026 Neil Thompson and Bernard Moss

The right of Neil Thompson and Bernard Moss to be identified as authors of this work has been asserted in accordance with sections 77 and 78 of the Copyright, Designs and Patents Act 1988.

All rights reserved. No part of this book may be reprinted or reproduced or utilised in any form or by any electronic, mechanical, or other means, now known or hereafter invented, including photocopying and recording, or in any information storage or retrieval system, without permission in writing from the publishers.

For Product Safety Concerns and Information please contact our EU representative GPSR@ taylorandfrancis.com. Taylor & Francis Verlag GmbH, Kaufingerstraße 24, 80331 München, Germany.

Trademark notice: Product or corporate names may be trademarks or registered trademarks, and are used only for identification and explanation without intent to infringe.

First edition published in 2020 by Avenue Media Solutions.

British Library Cataloguing-in-Publication Data
A catalogue record for this book is available from the British Library

ISBN: 978-1-041-16019-9 (hbk)
ISBN: 978-1-041-16012-0 (pbk)
ISBN: 978-1-003-68231-8 (ebk)

DOI: 10.4324/9781003682318

Typeset in Times New Roman
by codeMantra

Contents

Welcome!

… to *Spirituality and Religion in Human Services*, part of the *Practice Manuals for Busy Professionals* series. This manual has been developed partly to draw attention to the vitally important part spirituality and religion play in people's lives and partly to help students, practitioners and managers across the people professions, broadly defined, to explore how to ensure that such matters are appropriately taken into consideration in their work. It offers plenty of food for thought, with plenty of ideas and insights to help develop a well-informed approach to practice. In addition, it offers considerable practice guidance to help avoid common pitfalls and achieve best practice wherever possible.

Spirituality continues to be a 'hot' topic these days, with an extensive literature base. However, that literature is polarized, in the sense that much of it is academic and specialized at one extreme, while at the other, there is a glut of populist 'dumbed-down' literature that does not do justice to the complexities involved. This manual aims to bridge the gap by providing a text that will appeal to students, practitioners and managers across a wide range of people professions.

One of the overall aims of the manual is to provide a sound foundation of understanding of spirituality as an important phenomenon in its own right, related to, but distinct from, religion. There is a tendency to equate spirituality with religion. In reality, though, religion is just one way of expressing spirituality and fulfilling spiritual needs. People who have no religious faith affiliation also have spiritual needs and, indeed, many religious people do not necessarily have their spiritual needs met through their religion. All these complexities have implications for professional practice, hence the need for a practice manual like this. Basically, our aim is to promote what Canda *et al.* (2020) call 'spiritually sensitive practice'.

We also explore why it is important to take account of those circumstances where faith of some kind is part of the life of the individuals involved.

About the authors

Neil Thompson is a highly experienced award-winning author and educator with over 50 books to his name in the academic and professional fields, with an excellent reputation for covering complex issues clearly and accessibly without oversimplifying them. His online academy offers Chartered Management Institute qualifications in leadership as well as a wide range of other courses. He has held full or honorary professorships at four UK universities and is currently a visiting professor at the Open University and Wrexham University. He has over 45 years' experience in the helping professions as a practitioner, manager, educator and consultant. In 2011 he was presented with a Lifetime Achievement Award by BASW Cymru, the Wales branch of the British Association of Social Workers. In 2014, he was presented with the Dr Robert Fulton award for Excellence in the field of Death, Dying and Bereavement from the Center for Death Education and Bioethics at the University of Wisconsin-La Crosse in the United States. He works with Vigoroom, a highly sophisticated employee wellness platform to host an online Centre of Excellence for leaders of all kinds to complement the Chartered Management Institute leadership qualifications he offers. His website, with his highly acclaimed *Manifesto for Making a Difference*, is at www. NeilThompson.info.

Bernard Moss was Emeritus Professor of Social Work Education and Spirituality at Staffordshire University, where he began working with social work students in 1993. His particular teaching interests focused on communication skills, studies in death, dying and bereavement, and mediation studies. He was formerly

Director of the Centre for Spirituality and Health at Staffordshire University and made significant contributions to debates on this important theme. In 2004 he was awarded a National Teaching Fellowship by the Higher Education Academy to mark his teaching excellence, and he became a Senior Fellow in 2007. He was a founding member of the British Association for the Study of Spirituality (now the International Network for the Study of Spirituality). Bernard's earlier career included roles as a probation officer, relationship counsellor, mediator and leader of a faith community. Sadly, he passed away while the first edition of this manual was being prepared.

Foreword

When the authors of this book trained as social workers, considerable emphasis was placed on understanding the nature and values of social work and on the social worker understanding themselves. As social work educators, Neil Thompson and Bernard Moss were among the first cohort of social work academics who were required to implement a competency-based model of learning. This handbook brings together the essence of the approach of both authors – that knowledge, values and skills cannot be separated when working with human beings in what was once termed the 'helping professions', or, as currently known, 'human services'. This is no 'how to' manual but an in-depth exploration of the huge topics of spirituality and religion which seeks to actively engage the reader in a reflective journey. It methodically examines both topics, in such a way (as the Epilogue wryly acknowledges) that 'huge themes' and 'complex and contentious issues' are addressed on the way. It is this that gives integrity to the third part, 'Making a difference'.

Religion and spirituality have had a tricky ride in human services. From historical origins closely linked to religious and charitable foundations, the transition to becoming secular professions led to a distancing from those origins, and sometimes, a suspicion of religion as the source of problems for many troubled individuals. Practitioners with a strong faith often felt themselves divided between the beliefs and moral imperatives of their religion and the ideological direction of travel in their profession. Yet gradually, the challenges of working in multicultural contexts and across age groups meant that even practitioners with a determinedly secular mindset had to acknowledge that many people do not see the world in the same way and that their, very different, 'worldview' springs from their religious or spiritual affiliation; further, that this might be hugely significant in how these individuals and families deal with life's challenges. At the same time, a growing body of research began to suggest, and seek to evidence, that there might be more contributing to health and wellbeing than psychosocial understandings, including for people of no religion. Thus, the term, 'spiritual but not religious', slipped into the professional lexicon, only to be challenged after decades of use by writers claiming that this is a western philosophical construct that has no meaning for anyone who does not live in a highly secularized society or who comes from a marginalized culture within such societies.

So, how to understand and interact with religion and spirituality in the everyday demands of human services practice today is complex and contentious. Small wonder that many practitioners continue to plead that they are not equipped to deal with the spiritual dimension, that they do not even know where to start. Yet they deal constantly with people struggling with loss, oppression, abuse and disadvantage – situations in which a person's internal resources may be crucial in finding healing and recovery and external resources may be few or inadequate. Helping the other person to connect with their spiritual resources, internal and external and from whatever source, is an important but often neglected dimension of empowerment.

Neil Thompson and Bernard Moss have lived and worked through much of this turbulent journey. They are distinguished by being in the vanguard of researchers and educators who have grappled with the task of bringing spirituality and religion back into the professional discourse and developing tools to assist practitioners. That they have done so from very different personal belief systems – Thompson as an existentialist and Moss as a Christian minister – greatly enhances the perspective of this book.

Bernard Moss sadly died as the first edition of this manual was being finalized. Coming five years after his death, this second edition demonstrates a careful curation of his body of work, in which Neil Thompson manages to seamlessly update without losing the integrity of both authors' voices. Chapters addressing the complexity of moral foundations in pluralistic societies and of the political challenges posed to and by religion are timely, as we reflect on the global turbulence in both those arenas over the last five years. This, and an honest consideration of factors which inhibit the development and nurturing of spirituality, exemplify the lifelong vocation of Moss and Thompson to open up '... a new way of "knowing", fit for purpose when facing [contemporary] challenges' (Holloway and Moss, 2010, p. 183).

Margaret Holloway
Emeritus Professor, the University of Hull

Preface to the second edition

When Bernard Moss passed away early in 2020 we were in the process of working together on two parallel projects, both involving taking some of our earlier published work, updating it, extending it by adding new materials and reorganizing it into a practice manual format – that is, texts that were academically sound and well informed, while also being of practical use to a wide variety of people across the people professions (by which we mean the human services broadly defined, as well as management and human resources – in fact, any setting where success depends on helping people address their problems and fulfil their potential).

The first of those two ventures was published as *The Values-based Practice Manual* (Moss and Thompson, 2020, second edition, 2026). What you are now reading is the second of those ventures. They were two separate projects, but have much in common, as values have spiritual implications and roots, while spirituality incorporates values as well as beliefs.

With permission from Russell House Publishing, this second project includes some of Bernard's original work which was published in *Spirituality and Religion* which was part of Russell House Publishing's 'Theory into Practice' series, for which I was the series editor. I have rearranged and updated his work and added extensively to it, being careful at all times to make sure that what I wrote was consistent with Bernard's approach and understanding. The same applies to this updated and extended second edition, including the three new chapters that have been added.

Bernard and I had different starting points when it came to spirituality and religion. Bernard was an ordained minister, while my approach is rooted in atheistic existentialism. However, despite these different launch pads, we very quickly found ourselves in strong agreement about:

(i)   All people have spiritual needs and face spiritual challenges in terms of developing and sustaining meaning, purpose and direction and a sense of who they are and how they fit into the world. This is regardless of whether or not they are members of faith communities or have religious beliefs – religion is a common basis for spirituality, but it is not the only one.
(ii) All professional work that involves getting to know people and their needs must take account of spiritual and, where relevant, religious concerns. These are not marginal concerns that can be largely ignored – they are at the core of what it means to be a human being. They play a highly significant part in shaping our sense of who we are and how we fit into the world.

Bernard and I were also very much in agreement that neglecting these issues is highly problematic, albeit not uncommon. Our objective in developing this manual has therefore been to provide a basis of understanding and guidance to support students, practitioners and managers in making sure that matters of spirituality and religion are given the full attention they deserve and from a suitably well-informed position.

The manual is based on three key points of principle:

1.   We are neither promoting religious belief nor disparaging it. We leave it up to you to make your own mind up and explore your own path.
2.   It is important, in working in the people professions, that we recognize and address people's spiritual needs, whether or not these are expressed in religious terms.
3.   As people engaged in challenging work, we can be empowered by taking our own spiritual needs seriously.

These are complex, contentious and sensitive issues, and so there can be no simple formulas to follow or straightforward answers to the difficult questions posed. However, there is much that can be done to help make sure we are well equipped to rise to the challenges involved – this manual is intended to play a part in developing the knowledge, skills and confidence to make a success of that venture.

Dr Neil Thompson

'The word *spirituality* may not speak to those who dwell chiefly in the intellect or those who equate the word with organized religion. If you prefer to think of spirituality as simply believing in connection, that's fine. If you choose to think of it as believing in magic, that's fine too. The things we believe carry a charge regardless of whether they can be proven or not.

The practice of spirituality is a way of looking at a world where you're not alone. There are deeper meanings behind the surface. The energy around you can be harnessed to elevate your work. You are part of something much larger than can be explained – a world of immense possibilities.'

(Rubin, 2025, p. 32)

Introduction

It has been drilled into students in a number of disciplines for many years now that 'self-location' is an essential ingredient in their reflective practice (Thompson and Moss, 2026). It makes a big difference whether you practise from a male or female perspective; or from a black, Asian or white point of view; whether your sexuality is LGTBQ+ or straight, and whether you see the world from a disabled or non-disabled perspective. The central issue is that who we are and where we come from fundamentally affect our values, assumptions and perspectives. We owe it to others to make this as clear as we can, to help them in their own explorations, rather than assume that we have achieved some sort of fully objective detachment in communicating eternal truths. There may be some people, of course, who feel that it is possible, and desirable, that such issues are taught in an objective, dispassionate way, and who feel that the value base of the teacher or author can be sufficiently muted in order to achieve objectivity. We have to say, however, that we cannot agree with this position.

We therefore feel that it is important for you, as you make your way through this manual, to know a little of where we are coming from, so that you can interpret what we have to say accordingly. Being white, we cannot hope to do full justice to a black perspective – although we can operate on the basis of an anti-racist perspective. Being male, we cannot hope to do full justice to a female perspective – although we can adopt an anti-sexist perspective. Being heterosexual, and cisgender we cannot hope to do full justice to LGBTQ+ perspectives – but we can do our best to address heterosexism and related forms of discrimination. These are complex, contentious and sensitive issues, and religion has long been implicated in oppressive practices, and so we should not expect simple or straightforward answers. There will be plenty of dilemmas along the way, such is the nature of the topics we will be covering.

DOI: 10.4324/9781003682318-1

We cannot hope to do full justice to those who belong to various faith communities, or to those who feel more at home with the label of humanist, atheist or agnostic – and with so much Christian imperialism to cope with, we can understand if much of what we say is treated, by some at least, with more than healthy scepticism.

But, we all have to be true to ourselves and to speak the truth as we perceive it. From where we are coming from, the issues of religion and spirituality take us to the very heart of what it means to be human and to be living together in society. For us, there are profound connections across religion, spirituality and social justice; between the foundation stone of compassion and the human rights of those who are marginalized, oppressed and victimized. They are of deep significance, in our opinion, and deserve to be taken seriously by anyone who is a member of the people professions.

Not that this is necessarily one-way traffic. In matters to do with religion and spirituality, there has been a perceived hostility towards some Christian and Muslim students, who have felt that their faith commitment was being devalued by both academic staff and other students on their professional courses (Channer, 1998). Many curricula, for example, have often dealt with these issues through neglect, much to the consternation of students who come from faith communities and who wish to explore the relationship between their faith-based values and their professional values. There is certainly a feeling in some disciplines that to raise issues of religion and spirituality is to go against the tide of contemporary professional education. But the tide has begun to turn (see, for example, Hodge et al., 2024).

We both have a passionate interest in these vital topics. We believe that, at their best, they are liberating and life enhancing and should take their rightful place within the practice curriculum and be taken seriously by everyone involved as part of best practice. That same commitment to best practice, however, will also be active in recognizing and challenging areas where religion and spirituality have become oppressive in the lives of the individuals, families and groups that people professionals are engaged with.

In this manual, we propose that spirituality may be understood as what we do to give expression to our chosen worldview. We hope that this definition will prove 'fit for purpose' as we explore these crucial issues and seek to relate them to our professional practice.

> We shall not cease from exploration,
> And the end of all our exploring
> Will be to arrive where we started
> And know the place for the first time.
>
> (T.S. Eliot, 'Little Gidding', *Four Quartets*, lines 239–242)

Setting the scene

'If I were you, I wouldn't start from here!'

This jocular riposte, occasionally offered to the bewildered traveller struggling to reach a destination without reliable signposts, captures something of the dilemma about how to begin a manual about spirituality and religion. For some, the very title may be off-putting: this is territory that feels distinctly uncomfortable and unfamiliar, and even to ask for directions causes them some consternation or unease. For others, there may be a contrasting sense of excitement precisely because this is familiar territory, and they feel very much at home here, and secretly wish that many more would join them.

Already we see that the danger of polarization has been raised in the opening paragraph, with some people feeling that this is definitely not for them, while others warmly welcome the enterprise. This should come as no surprise, for these are topics that are notorious for setting people's teeth on edge, and not just at parties. In the professional training courses designed to prepare people for a career as people professionals, it is as likely as not that the issues of spirituality and religion will either receive scant attention or be relegated to the domain of personal interests or hobbies, like rock climbing or choral singing:

> If that is your scene, then go for it if you must, but don't bring it into your professional life – there are other professionals whose job it is to deal with those issues: they have no place in the contemporary practitioner's toolkit.

Part of the difficulty in starting such a discussion is precisely this pre-existing polarization that seems to be set on predetermined train lines of thought – occasionally, there may be some parallel journeys where people can call across to each other, but more often than not, the train lines go off in different directions, or achieve the buffeting and disconcerting effect as two trains hurtle past each other in opposite directions. No wonder these subjects tend to be avoided. As we observed at the outset, 'if I were you, I wouldn't start from here'.

But times are changing. Within the nursing sphere, the spiritual and religious needs of patients have long been recognized, with multi-faith chaplaincies increasingly being established. In the sphere of social work education, the need for social workers to take issues of religion and spirituality seriously has begun to be recognized (Holloway and Moss, 2010).

Whatever the particular emphasis of the work – be it youth and community work; criminal or community justice; counselling; advice work; social work, nursing or health care; policing; prison-based work; management across all sectors; or human resources practice – there will be occasions when issues of religion and spirituality need not only to be recognized, but also taken seriously in the multicultural, multi-faith societies of the UK and beyond.

This manual therefore offers an introduction for a wide range of people professionals who recognize the importance of taking these issues seriously, whatever their own personal 'take' on them may be. Its starting point is a celebration of diversity and the need to treat others with dignity and respect, especially when views and opinions differ widely. This is not the place, however, for a debate about the relative merits of the claims to 'ultimate truth' made by some religions. Readers who wish to explore the apologetics for a particular religion will need to undertake this as a distinctly separate enterprise. Nevertheless, an important dimension of the manual is a discussion about the extent to which religion and spirituality are perceived as having an emancipatory/liberating/life-enhancing effect or a negative/oppressive/life-denying impact upon people's lives, and this will inevitably involve a range of value judgements on the part of the authors and the readers. Whether we like it or not, we will find that we are being drawn into subjective evaluations as professional workers when we start taking these issues seriously for ourselves and for those we work with.

It is worth adding a brief note about a phrase that will be used in this manual. Faith-based organizations (FBOs) is a phrase that seeks to be comprehensive and inclusive in its scope. Admittedly less elegant than its synonym 'faith communities', it is nevertheless a useful term designed to include the wide variety of religious groupings and meeting places for worship and community outreach. In that sense, it has a wider scope than faith communities because it will include community-based initiatives that may be separate from the worship-based activities of, for example, churches or mosques. It is also worth noting that we use the term 'religion' in the singular to denote a powerful social force in both a historic and contemporary context. However, we need to acknowledge that the reality of religion is plural – that is, there are very many religions. Indeed, it is estimated that, in addition to such major religions as Christianity, Islam, Judaism, Hinduism, Sikhism, Buddhism, Bahá'í Faith, Jainism, Shinto and Taoism, there are thousands of other religions globally. Our focus, however, is on the commonalities of religion as a social force and influence on people's lives, rather than its differences and distinctions (but see Chapter 17 for a discussion of religious diversity).

An interesting development to note since the publication of the first edition of this manual is the level of interest shown in its subject matter by people in management and leadership roles. It has become apparent that the changing world of work, with its increased pressures and complexities, has created new challenges (Cheese, 2021). These challenges can be seen to have a strong spiritual dimension, as we shall explore later. So, it can be acknowledged that this manual has much to offer not only members of the human services broadly defined but also managers and leaders across all sectors.

The manual is in three parts. In Part I, we focus on spirituality and present it as part of human existence closely linked to religion, but also an important consideration for those people who have no religious affiliations or beliefs. We build our comments around two acronyms: IMPACT (which is something spirituality clearly has in so many ways) and WINDOWS (representing the way different spiritualities give us different perspectives or 'windows on the world').

In Part II, we focus on religion and explore its significance for many people's lives. A key message we want to put forward is that, regardless of our own views on religion, we need to be able to tune in to what religion means to the people we serve or support in some way. We have to be able to put our own views in abeyance and pay close attention to the significance of faith in people's lives. Consequently, in Part II, we discuss some of the subtleties and complexities of religion to help you be better equipped to address the issues that are likely to arise. Given that spirituality is a major part of religion, much of what we will have discussed in Part I will be relevant here too.

In Part III, we examine a range of topics that spirituality and religion have a bearing on in one or more ways. Our aim is to highlight how many of the issues we have discussed in Parts I and II can be of practical value in relation to making a positive difference to people's lives. The range of topics covered is not exhaustive, of course, but should be sufficient to provide a helpful platform of understanding.

NB Interspersed throughout the text are key points, tips and 'Reflective Moments', by which we mean questions about your own views and experiences to help you link the broader issues to your own unique personal circumstances. In addition, each chapter ends with an exercise. We strongly encourage you to pay attention to these, as they will be useful in getting you thinking about the important issues covered.

Spirituality

Introduction to Part I

Some concepts are fairly easy to define and simple to explain, while others are quite complex and 'slippery'. Spirituality clearly comes into the latter category. But, we will not let that deter us from emphasizing its importance and examining it in some detail. Despite this slipperiness, we hope that you will have a much clearer picture of what spirituality is all about by the time you reach the end of Part I.

It can be helpful to consider spirituality as providing:

> a context for exploring some fundamental existential questions; and ... also raises sociological questions about our obligations not only to ourselves but also 'to the wider realm of families, community and society' [Cox and Thompson, 2020a, p. 7].
>
> (Moss, 2020, p. 167)

Spirituality is a multidimensional phenomenon, and so to make sure that we cover as many aspects of it as we reasonably can in the space available, we use two related frameworks, IMPACT and WINDOWS. These are acronyms, spelling out a total of 13 different dimensions of spirituality, 13 elements that go to make up this vitally important aspect of human experience.

IMPACT stands for:

Identity – Who we are and how we fit into the wider world.
Meaning – Our constant struggle to understand and make sense.
Purpose – Our attempts to answer 'why' questions and set goals.

DOI: 10.4324/9781003682318-2

Awe and wonder – Marvelling at the amazing world we live in.
Connectedness – The sense of being part of something bigger than ourselves.
Transcendence – Going beyond or rising above everyday mundane reality.

WINDOWS stands for:

Wisdom – Making appropriate use of knowledge, understanding and experience.
Integrity – Being aware of our values and living in accordance with them.
Nurturance – Recognizing that we can make our interactions positive or negative.
Direction – Being committed to doing something meaningful with our lives.
Openness to experience and learning – Embracing our vulnerability.
Wellbeing – Our quality of life.
Security – Feeling safe and comfortable 'in our own skin'.

Of course, these 13 elements are not completely distinct from one another; they blend into each other in places and interact in significant ways. We should therefore see these two frameworks not as static models but as representations of a set of complex dynamics, constantly interacting and shaping our lives and our experience.

We shall shortly explore each of these dimensions in turn to help you develop a fuller picture of what each one of them means and how and why they are significant. But first, we feel it is important to be clear about what we mean by spirituality. It is an extremely difficult concept to pin down, with very many definitions having been offered over time. Rather than lose the practical focus of this manual by devoting pages to possible ways of defining spirituality, we shall offer a very straightforward one. For us, spirituality is *what we do to give expression to our chosen worldview* (Holloway and Moss, 2010). Our worldview is, in effect, a set of filters based on our experiences and our values through which we make sense of our lives as they unfold.

There are two significant aspects of this. First, we say 'give expression to' because we see this as a key foundation of spirituality. In discussing spirituality, we are generally exploring how we express ourselves as people, how we engage with the world as functioning human beings and make sense of it. Second, we use the term 'worldview' because we recognize that we do not all see the world in the same way. Much will depend on our upbringing and the social context in which that takes place as well as – importantly – how we react to and make sense of that upbringing.

For many, of course, that worldview will be shaped by adherence to a particular faith and will be expressed in part at least through religious practices. However, we are increasingly seeing reference to the idea of being 'spiritual but not religious', by which is meant seeking spiritual fulfilment outside of a religious context. For many people of faith, this is anathema, as their worldview is based on the idea of one true faith. By contrast, the Dalai Lama, a world-renowned spiritual leader, is on record as saying that religion is not necessary for spirituality to flourish. What is important, he argues, is for our inner values not to be neglected: 'What we need today is an approach to ethics which makes no recourse to religion and can be equally acceptable to those with faith and those without: a secular ethics' (2011, pp. xiii-xiv).

We hope that the following diagram will clarify and help you to appreciate the view of religion and spirituality we are adopting here (Figure 0.1).

People in the top-left-hand quadrant will be those who have a religious faith that meets their spiritual needs. However, not all people of faith are in such a fortunate position. For a variety of reasons, some people will not have their spiritual needs met through their religion, even though they are believers. These are people we would assign to the lower-left-hand box.

The top-right-hand quadrant is where we would find the people who designate themselves as 'spiritual but not religious'. In the lower-right-hand box, we will find very many people who achieve no solace through religion but are not able to find peace or fulfilment without it either – in some sense, perhaps, victims of a fast-paced materialistic world that does more to alienate them than to engage or inspire them.

For centuries, there have been debates along the horizontal axis of the diagram, raising the question of the existence or otherwise of God. What concerns us more in this manual is the vertical axis – that is, how can we do our best to help people find spiritual fulfilment, whether through religion or other means?

We see this question (and the issues it raises) not in addition to the everyday duties of people professionals, but as a fundamental dimension of those duties. If we are leaving spiritual matters out of the picture, how can we hope to support, protect or empower people in the challenges they face?

Where people draw spiritual nourishment through religious faith, there is much that people professionals can do to help them draw on those resources

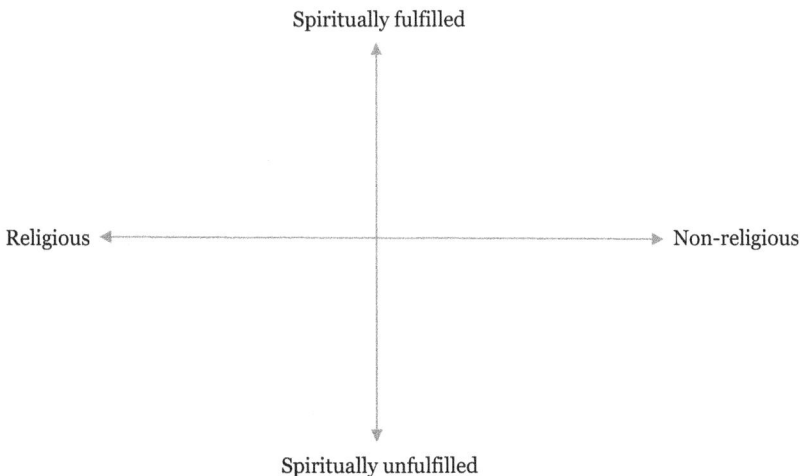

Figure 0.1 Spiritual fulfilment

when they need to. However, in an interesting account of non-religious spirituality, Hägglund (2019) writes of the value of what he calls 'secular faith':

> The sense of finitude – the sense of the ultimate fragility of everything we care about – is at the heart of what I call *secular faith*. To have secular faith is to be devoted to a life that will end, to be dedicated to projects that can fail or break down. Ranging from the concrete (how we approach funerals) to the general (what makes a life worth living). ... secular faith expresses itself in the ways we mourn our loved ones, make commitments, and care about a sustainable world. I call it *secular* faith because it is devoted to a form of life that is bounded by time.
>
> (pp. 5–6)

This means that, regardless of where people are located on the horizontal axis, we can play an important part in helping them to achieve spiritual fulfilment on the vertical axis and to draw on the resources their faith (religious or secular) offers them.

CHAPTER 1

Identity

Introduction

Our sense of who we are and how we fit into the world is crucial to our sense of wellbeing, spiritual fulfilment and personal development. Major changes in society in relation to social expectations around gender, ethnicity, sexuality and age have thrown issues of social identity into sharp relief. This raises important issues for the aspect of spirituality that is concerned with who we are and how we fit into the world and our 'connectedness'. These issues are particularly important in the context of a world in which religious approaches to spirituality are increasingly being complemented, if not replaced, by non-religious approaches.

If religion is no longer providing as fully as it used to for many people the clarity of expectations in relation to identity, and social changes have also 'muddied the water' around questions of selfhood, what role is there for a non-religious spirituality to provide guidance and a framework of understanding?

From the point of view of the people professions, it is also vitally important to recognize that the people who are needing help and support may benefit in many cases from assistance in establishing clarity about identity. For example, the significance of spirituality in relation to mental health problems is achieving growing prominence.

Traditionally, issues of identity have been considered mainly in psychological terms. While there clearly are psychological aspects of identity, we should not forget that there are also significant social aspects and, what is particularly important for present purposes, spiritual aspects too. Our sense of self will owe a great deal to our 'social location' – that is, how we fit into the wider context of life in terms of such matters as class, ethnicity, gender, religion, language group and so on. All these factors are key influences on us as we grow up,

DOI: 10.4324/9781003682318-3

and their interactions play a major part in shaping the identity aspect of our spirituality.

For an individual to have some sense of who they are, they will need to have at least some sense of meaning, purpose and direction, which are clearly spiritual matters. If we return to our definition of spirituality as how a person expresses their chosen worldview, then it should also be clear that our identity and our worldview will be closely intertwined. Our sense of who we are will shape our worldview and our worldview will shape our sense of who we are.

The role of religion in shaping identity can range from having no impact at all, through having some influence to varying degrees, to being a major factor. Some people, for example, have a sense of divine calling, and so their identity is closely linked to their perceived relationship with a higher power (Hamm et al., 2024). This can be particularly significant when someone loses their faith – for example, when Richard Holloway, formerly a bishop, reached the point where he could no longer remain committed to the Christian faith (Holloway, 2005). The relationship between religion and identity is therefore both complex and significant.

It is also important to note that identity is relatively fluid, in the sense that the commonsense notion that individuals have a fixed personality that remains the same throughout life does not fit with the much more complex reality of identity formation and maintenance. For example, for a significant proportion of people, religion is a key part of their identity, but the Pew Research Center (2025) points out that many people, especially Christians and Buddhists, are changing their religious beliefs.

In *Values-Based Practice* (Thompson and Moss, 2026), we emphasize the importance of 'self-location' – that is, the value of being clear about your own sense of who you are and how you fit into the wider world, especially in relation to such matters as class, ethnicity and gender that will have a significant impact in terms of the potential for being discriminated against, marginalized or treated as 'other'. If you have not already achieved that clarity, we strongly suggest you do that now, as it can be very helpful in terms of tuning in to your own spirituality and that, in turn, can make you more sensitive to, and understanding of, other people's spiritual needs and challenges.

People will often feel confused about their identity at certain significant moments in their life – for example, when they have experienced a major loss (see Chapter 25 below) or been abused (which, of course, involves a number of losses). Consequently, issues around identity are not limited to working with adolescents. People with mental health problems can struggle to feel comfortable with their own sense of self, in large part because of the stigma and discrimination that is sadly still prevalent in relation to such matters. In addition, older people can at times struggle to retain a strong sense of self while aspects of their life that they have felt comfortable and secure with begin to slip away from them – for example, as a result of retirement or losing an ability due to age-related infirmity or, indeed, as a result of the demeaning consequences of ageism (Sue Thompson, 2025; Thompson and Cox, 2025).

> **Key point**
>
> There are two important sides to identity: first, the importance of your own identity and how it is shaping the way you see the world; and, second, how the identity of the person(s) you are working with is shaping their sense of reality. This gives us a strong basis for empathy, compassion and mutual understanding.

Challenging essentialism

One very important concept to consider in relation to identity is 'essentialism'. This refers to the common mistake of assuming that we each have a 'true essence', a 'real self' that is unchanging over time. This highly oversimplified understanding of identity is problematic because it acts as an obstacle to change, growth and development. The idea that 'I am who I am and I can't change' simply does not fit with reality, where examples of people changing – often changing quite significantly – are not too difficult to find.

Counsellors and other therapists will often find themselves having to gently and constructively challenge such essentialist views that are proving to be self-disempowering and thereby shutting off avenues to growth, problem-solving, trauma recovery or whatever the issues may be for the individual concerned. Helping to free people up from such self-limiting views can be immensely empowering in bringing about positive change. This can also be an issue for managers in relation to promoting personal and professional development in their staff.

There is therefore much to be gained by giving some thought to identity and how it evolves over time as a key part of spirituality. Taking account of such matters can enrich the quality of our work and be more effective in bringing about the changes needed to make progress in whatever plans we are trying to put into practice.

Of course, it would be unrealistic and counterproductive to be constantly thinking about our own identity and that of the people we engage with, but giving the issues some thought when we need to is likely to be not only more realistic, but also more empowering in terms of achieving our goals as people professionals.

> **Exercise 1**
>
> What do you see as the key factors in your life that have shaped your sense of who you are? Think about this in terms of both wider social factors (class, gender, ethnicity and so on) as well as experiences that are specific to you as an individual. What do you feel you can learn about yourself and your spirituality by considering these issues?

CHAPTER 2

Meaning

Introduction

The existential challenges of finding and creating meaning and having a sense of purpose and direction are significant elements of spirituality. This chapter explores how these can be addressed, with or without religion.

For centuries, religion has been a major source of people's sense of meaning, purpose and direction. Does this mean that the increasing number of people who eschew religious faith are doomed to a meaningless life without purpose? The discussion here draws on existentialist philosophy to answer that question in the negative. In existentialist terms, life is inherently meaningful. As Merleau-Ponty (2013) put it, we are 'condemned to meaning'. So, what options are there with or without religion for creating meaning, purpose and direction? This chapter seeks to begin to answer that question.

As human beings we are meaning-making creatures. That is, whatever circumstances we may find ourselves in, we will seek to make the situation meaningful; we will try to make sense of it. This is why we find some situations frustrating when we can't make sense of them – for example, when somebody has acted out of character, and so what has happened does not initially make sense to us until we can find out more about what brought about that particular action.

Narratives

A key concept here is that of 'narrative' which is the technical term for how we live our lives through stories. We create meanings by developing stories that fit our understanding (our chosen worldview) and thereby help us make sense of any given situation. So, when someone does act out of character, we may learn that they have been under a lot of stress lately, so we develop a narrative

DOI: 10.4324/9781003682318-4

accordingly – the story in our mind becomes one in which the person concerned acted in an uncharacteristic way because of the adverse influence of stress.

Consequently, when we want to understand a person's spirituality (and perhaps why they are not spiritually fulfilled) so that we are better placed to help them, it can be very helpful to try to identify the narrative they are adopting – in effect, to see the world through their eyes. Your own narrative may be very different from theirs.

'Narrative therapy' is a well-established approach to helping people address their problems and challenges and to help them grow. It involves working closely with them to clarify the narrative they are using and, where this is a self-disempowering narrative, seeking to renegotiate a more positive and empowering one. An example of a disempowering narrative would be where someone who is struggling with depression adopts a defeatist attitude, focuses on the negatives of their situation and disregards the positives. It would be characterized by the notion that 'I am trapped'. A skilled worker using narrative therapy could help to move towards a more balanced approach that weighs up both the positives and the negatives and explores possible ways forward that would not otherwise have been considered.

Working with someone who is overly anxious would be another example. Their 'narrative' is telling them that they are in more danger than is actually the case. Narrative therapy can be used to help develop a more balanced approach to risk and danger.

Reflective moment

Imagine you are needing help from a professional or from your manager and, while they are clearly trying to be helpful, they are just not seeing the situation from your point of view – they do not appreciate where you are coming from. How is that likely to make you feel and how effective do you feel their efforts to be supportive are likely to be?

Why?

A helpful way of understanding meaning is to think of it as our attempt to keep answering the question 'why?': Why is this happening? Why do I feel like I do? Why are things changing? and so on. This takes us back to existentialism and, in particular, to Viktor Frankl's classic text, *Man's Search for Meaning*, in which he argues that being human means being responsible for your own existence. In other words, Frankl sees the search for meaning as the making of a response. In these terms, 'man's search for meaning' is not the conscious intellectual making of meaning – as Frankl puts it: 'the spiritual basis of human existence ... is ultimately unconscious' (p. 37) – it is a search for a response to life: how shall I live?

But it is not necessarily about finding *the* answer, as if life were some sort of puzzle. It is more about finding or creating answers that make sense in terms of who we are, our self-narrative to date and the social circumstances we find ourselves in.

A common misunderstanding of existentialism is that it is a philosophy of meaninglessness, but this could not be further from the truth. Certainly, existentialism in most of its forms rejects any sort of absolute, ultimate or predefined meaning. But, we cannot conclude from this that life is without meaning. Rather, it is a case of recognizing that *the meaning of life is making meaning.* As Foley (2011) puts it: 'the search for meaning is itself the meaning, the Way is the destination, the quest is the grail' (p. 74).

We cannot escape meaning because whatever we do, wherever we go, we attach meaning to what happens and the circumstances in which it happens. It becomes part of our constantly developing narrative. In this sense, then, meaning is very much a spiritual matter, not necessarily in the sense of embracing a predefined meaning as religious teachings commonly expound, but by constantly making sense of our lives on a day-to-day basis. In this way, meaning can be understood as something we 'do' rather than something we 'have'.

One of the earliest existentialist thinkers, the Danish writer Søren Kierkegaard (1813–55), was a committed Christian, but he strongly challenged the idea that being devout simply involves following a set of religious precepts. In his view, it was more about finding your own way of living, making your own authentic choices and, in that way, being worthy in the eyes of God.

But, regardless of whether we embrace a predefined ultimate reality, it remains the case that we are constantly making meaning, forever writing the next chapter of our life narrative, as it were.

Exercise 2

If you were asked to explain your own life narrative, what would you say? What would you regard as the things in your life that give you meaning or, in a sense, give a shape to your life?

CHAPTER 2

CHAPTER 3

Purpose

Introduction

Having a sense of purpose is also something that is commonly associated with spirituality, often as part of the phrase 'meaning, purpose and direction'. A life without meaning, purpose and direction would generally be regarded as a fairly empty life spiritually. But, what do we actually mean by purpose and how does it fit with meaning and direction? Furthermore, what is its significance for people professionals seeking to support, protect and empower others?

There is a huge literature on the value and benefits of goal setting (see, for example, Dobson and Wilson, 2008). Having something to aim for is deemed to be a good thing, as it gives us a source of motivation and can give a degree of focus and structure to our lives. While this is something we would not at all disagree with, we need to understand purpose in the spiritual sense in a much broader way.

A key issue is the age-old question of what life is for. The common answer of 'life is for living' may be true, but it is not very helpful in taking our understanding further. This question takes us back to the idea of seeing meaning not simply as something that is a given, predefined for us, but more like 'work in progress' in which we are constantly living out our life narrative. Life purpose can be understood in parallel terms.

If life is a process of ongoing meaning making, then one answer (or set of answers) to the question of what is life for could be: What do you want it to be for? Now that you have it, what do you want to do with it? What do you want your narrative to be? Of course, that does not mean that we have full control over that narrative. A useful analogy would be that, while we may be in the driving seat on our journey, we still have to rely on our vehicle (our body) and the road system and traffic conditions (the sociopolitical context).

DOI: 10.4324/9781003682318-5

A huge and burgeoning life coaching industry has grown up around this type of answer. When the much older tradition of business coaching latched on to the idea that success in business very much depends on how successful you are in living your life, this gave birth to the idea of life coaching. This is the basis of self-empowerment.

How we answer the question of what (our) life is for will shape our worldview and will also depend on how we express our chosen worldview. Both sides to this, then, are clearly spiritual in nature and both are concerned with meaning and our life narrative, the ongoing story we create as we live our lives.

Losing a sense of purpose

It is very common for people to lose their sense of purpose at certain times in their lives. This can happen when people are traumatized and/or experience a major loss, whether death related or not. Indeed, any major change can provoke a crisis that revolves around a sense of purpose. This can be for positive reasons, such as when someone becomes a parent but in doing so becomes disorientated and unclear about where their life is now going. Or it can be for negative reasons, as in a situation in which a man whose sense of purpose derives very much from the pride he takes in being a good husband and father who finds himself facing a divorce, especially if the scenario includes his being denied access to his child(ren).

A sense of purpose can be lost suddenly, as in the examples we have just given, or can evolve over time. An example of the latter would be where someone who has been highly committed to their profession who now becomes steadily more disillusioned and, in effect, burnt out: a community nurse whose caseload is so great that there is not enough time to do the work safely and effectively; a manager who is forced to implement a policy they regard as unjust, unethical or unworkable; or a teacher strongly committed to anti-racist practice who finds the school's rhetoric about such matters is not matched by the reality and any attempts to bridge the gap are met with significant resistance.

Many of the problems people professionals encounter will be characterized by a loss of sense of purpose, either as a contributory factor or as a byproduct of other issues. Tuning in to issues related to purpose can therefore be an important part of making a difference in people's lives.

TIP! Asking someone directly what they see as their life purpose is likely to be met with some degree of bewilderment. It is too 'big' a question to be asked directly. What is much better is to engage them in conversation about their lives and from this gain some sense of what they see as their life purpose. One way of doing this is to talk about what motivates them, what drives them forward.

Direction

A concept closely related to purpose is that of direction. If purpose is about the question of what is life for, then direction is about where do I want to take my life or where should I be taking it.

Much will depend on the individual's social location. For example, someone from a socially and/or economically privileged background will have more options in terms of what direction they can take their life in compared with someone from an underprivileged background. This applies, amongst other things, to matters relating to career. Indeed, career prospects and plans are a common basis for people's sense of purpose and direction in life. And these are, of course, very dependent on social factors, as we are a long way away from the ideal of a totally free, open and equal world of work.

We shall return to the topic of spiritual direction later.

Age and direction

Another aspect of inequality arises in relation to age. A common aspect of ageism is the tendency to deny older people a sense of future, to talk as if their lives are already over, or very nearly (Sue Thompson, 2025). Anti-ageist practice needs to be based on the recognition that the rest of your life is the rest of your life, whether that is three months, three years or three decades. In working with older people, it is therefore essential that we do not make the discriminatory assumption that any sense of purpose or direction does not apply to them. In reality, maintaining a sense of purpose and direction can be a major source of wellbeing for older people, while assumptions, actions or inactions that have the effect of undermining any such sense of purpose and direction can be profoundly oppressive.

Maintaining a sense of purpose and direction can be a major challenge for people when they retire or leave the workforce for any other reason (such as parenthood, disability or being laid off).

Exercise 3

What do you see as the various factors that contribute to your sense of purpose? How might you be able to help others who are struggling to have a helpful sense of purpose?

CHAPTER 4

Awe and wonder

Introduction

The 'numinous', the sense of very special moments, is part of religious life, but religion does not have a monopoly on awe, wonder and a sense of the sacred. This chapter therefore explores sources of awe and wonder regardless of whether they have a connection with the divine and considers the role they play in offering a degree of spiritual fulfilment.

We also discuss the related concept of 'the sacred' and consider how a distinction between sacred and profane can not only exist outside of a religious context, but also be very significant socially, psychologically and, of course, spiritually.

We also include discussion of how social inequalities can serve to produce a significant imbalance in terms of opportunities for awe and wonder but cannot deny them altogether. This introduces another important spiritual concept, namely hope. The role of hope in circumstances of inequality and oppression is an important one.

A sense of wonder

We tend to associate awe and wonder with special moments that help us rise above the ordinariness of everyday life (see the discussion of transcendence below). For members of faith communities, these tend to be associated with the divine, manifestations of God's majesty, and the term 'the numinous' is used to describe such experiences. However, in keeping with our theme that religion is an important source of spirituality, but not the only one, we want to make the point that experiences of awe and wonder are available to everyone and not limited to a religious context.

DOI: 10.4324/9781003682318-6

The term 'mystery' is often associated with such experiences in an attempt to capture the inexplicable emotional power of such moments. For people professionals, this emotional power can be important – for example, as a source of motivation and inspiration. Numinous moments can also be a source of solace for people who are grieving or otherwise wrestling with significant emotional challenges.

Key point

Mental health problems, such as depression and anxiety, can have the effect of blunting or distorting our emotional responses, potentially resulting in difficulties in engaging with or appreciating awe and wonder. By the same token, engaging with awe and wonder can have a therapeutic effect in terms of mental wellbeing.

Sources of wonder

Many examples of awe and wonder arise from the natural world – vistas of outstanding natural beauty, a beautiful dawn or sunset and so on being prime examples. Others arise from specific events, albeit often with a nature theme again. Being present at the birth of a child would be an example of this. Hari (2018), in his discussion of factors contributing to depression, includes a sense of disconnection from the natural world, and it is easy to see how this fits in with the importance of awe and wonder for our spiritual fulfilment.

Norman uses the term 'sublime' and quotes Immanuel Kant's description of it:

> Bold, overhanging and … threatening rocks, thunderclouds piled up the vault of heaven, borne along with flashes and peals, volcanoes in all their violence and destruction, hurricanes leaving desolation in their track, the boundless ocean rising with rebellious force, the high waterfall of some mighty river, and the like, make our power of resistance of trifling moment in comparison with their might.
>
> [Kant 1952, p. 110]. (p. 21)

This fits well with the idea of awe and wonder being inherent in religious mystery but also going beyond that.

Awe and wonder can be evoked spontaneously in certain circumstances, but can also be deliberately invoked – for example, through such practices as Zen, Vedanta and transpersonal psychology. For example, in Zen, the concept of 'satori' is used to refer to a moment of enlightenment or awakening. It leads to a direct experience of emptiness (śūnyatā), where the usual boundaries of the self dissolve. This experience can engender a deep connection to the universe and thus a profound experience of the numinous (Starlyte, 2024) and a heightened sense of wellbeing (Gorelik, 2016). Zen practitioners need to be fully present and aware (for example, through meditation) to facilitate this sense of 'dissolution of the self'.

Reflective moment

What gives you a sense of wonder? How impoverished would your life be without these being available to you? Do you make full use of the opportunities?

Some numinous moments happen as a result of a ritual designed to evoke a particular response. For example, some religious rituals can be powerfully evocative, as in the case of funerals or memorial services. Such rituals are often reinforced by the power of music, and indeed music itself can be a source of awe, wonder and transcendence, as can poetry and art at times (Bist et al., 2024).

The sacred

This is another term traditionally associated with religion, but which, on closer examination, can be seen to apply in a secular context too. In its specifically religious sense, it refers to aspects of the world that are closely associated with the holy and thus worthy of special respect and veneration (consecrated ground in graveyards, for example), as distinct from the 'profane' or ordinary.

The term is now increasingly being used beyond its religious roots to refer to anything that is worthy of that same special respect. Human life, of course, is regarded as sacred by most – but sadly not all – people. Similarly, much of the child protection system is based on the inviolability of childhood, thereby attaching a degree of sacredness to the innocence of children in recognizing their need for protection from abuse.

Inequality

Being able to afford to travel the world and view its wonders clearly gives access to opportunities for awe and wonder that most people cannot afford. So, when it comes to the benefits of awe and wonder, it is not a level playing field. In addition, the negative effects of poverty, deprivation, discrimination and oppression can serve as obstacles to appreciate and draw on awe and wonder as sources of spiritual nourishment.

However, we should not make the mistake of assuming that awe and wonder are the exclusive property of the wealthy and powerful, but it does mean that opportunities can be limited in some ways. This raises two challenges for people professionals committed to empowerment: (i) reducing inequality and the obstacles it presents; and (ii) supporting people in finding and making use of whatever opportunities they can.

Hope

How we engage with the world depends a great deal on hope, in the sense that how we approach certain situations will differ depending on how hopeful we are about being able to achieve whatever it is we are setting out to do. Hope can be motivating, reassuring and affirming, while hopelessness can not only fail to motivate, but actually demotivate, in the sense of robbing people of the will to move forward in any positive way.

There is an interesting two-way relationship between awe and wonder and hope. They can inspire each other, but the absence of either can contribute to the absence of the other. Much of the work that is done in the people professions involves creating and building on hope, and so there is potential worth exploring for using awe and wonder as ways of sustaining hope and working towards positive outcomes – whether this is done in religious or secular terms.

A similar situation can be seen to apply in the workplace in relation to organizational culture. Cultures are powerful influences on thoughts, feelings and actions in the workplace (Thompson, 2025a). They can be positive and affirming, or, sadly, they can be characterized by negativity, defeatism and cynicism – in other words, hopelessness. This highlights the (spiritual) importance of leadership in shaping and sustaining cultures that generate hope and motivation, rather than negativity. We should therefore recognize that the term 'spiritual leader' should not be limited to senior figures in a faith-based communities.

Exercise 4

People from different religious, cultural or philosophical backgrounds will have different ideas about what is or is not sacred. In working with people from a different background from your own, how can you make sure that you are being sufficiently sensitive to different needs and perspectives?

CHAPTER 5

Connectedness

Introduction

This term refers to the importance of seeing ourselves as being part of something bigger than ourselves, connected to a wider meaning or purpose. Religion generally offers this by its very nature, but there are other ways of achieving it. The focus in this chapter is therefore on the various ways in which a strong sense of connection can be achieved by those who do not choose a religious path. This includes a wide range of factors we shall explore here.

We begin, though, by looking at the two senses of connectedness, specific and general.

Connectedness: specific and general

As a religious concept, connectedness refers to having a sense of being part of something much bigger than ourselves, linked to the notion of a higher power. This can be a personified higher power, as in God, Allah or whatever, or a more impersonal one, such as 'the Life Force' of which George Bernard Shaw wrote. However, there also exist non-religious wider entities that can give the same sense of connectedness – for example, commitment to a particular political party or cause or humanitarian endeavour.

Connectedness, in this narrow specific sense, is something that gives us a meaningful set of connections to not only like-minded people but also to what these connections stand for, their symbolic power and sense of belonging in terms of a faith community and/or some other driving force in our lives.

However, we can also have a more general sense of connectedness as part of our humanity. This too can be religious ('We are all God's children') or secular in terms of a shared sense of human endeavour. Whether specific or general,

DOI: 10.4324/9781003682318-7

religious or secular, connectedness helps to give 'shape' to our lives, can be important for our identity and our sense of purpose and direction.

It reflects the sociological concept, drawn from the work of Pierre Bourdieu, of 'social capital' (Bourdieu, 2021). Just as financial capital refers to our economic resources, social capital refers to our *social* resources in terms of quality and quantity of relationships, institutional connections and so on. The more connected we are, the greater the opportunities for gaining spiritual value from our 'capital'.

> **TIP!** Do not underestimate the power or significance of connectedness. People will often not appreciate how much connectedness means to them until a particular connection or set of connections is lost or threatened.

Sources of connection

People can benefit considerably from the spiritual value of connectedness, and so it is worth giving some thought to some of the main ways in which a strong sense of connectedness can be achieved. The following should be a helpful, but far from comprehensive, selection:

■ Environmental concerns are a growing source of connectedness. As the threat to our habitat grows and the awareness of the need to act promptly and in significant ways becomes more well established, more and more people are engaging in 'green' issues (consider the popularity of Extinction Rebellion as a social movement, for example). Deep ecology is the term used to refer to the view of environmental factors as closely intertwined with other aspects of how society works, recognizing that environmentalism needs to be more than simply a 'tightening of our belts' when it comes to energy use. Deep ecology is based on the argument that changes need to be much more radical if we are serious about halting the destruction of our habitat, contending that our materialistic industrialized (and industrializing) societies are inherently wasteful of natural resources, in so far as they encourage consumption of those resources. Concern for the environment can therefore very clearly be seen as a significant source of connectedness for a large and growing number of people.

■ Political engagement of various kinds is commonly a significant source of connectedness. This can relate to particular parties as well as to cross-party or extra-party activities. An example of a cross-party cause might be a range of people from different parties who share a common commitment to a particular theme or set of issues, such as the development of proportional representation to replace the first-past-the-post system. An example of what we mean by a non-party cause might be a campaign to promote mental health awareness that has been organized without reference to, or involvement of, political parties. Of course, political matters can prove very divisive and set people against one another, but they also play a significant role in bring-ing people together in meaningful and empowering ways, as is evidenced by the positive role of trade unionism.

■ Public service, whether in paid employment or on a voluntary basis, is yet another source of connectedness for a significant number of people. Of course, some employees who work in a public service will see their job as purely a way of earning a living and will not have any sense of connected-ness beyond being a member of a team (and maybe not even in that way). However, for a significant proportion of people who work in a public service context, there will be a sense of attachment to the very notion of public service – for example, a sense of pride in being part of a network of services that are of value to the general public or particular subsections of the popula-tion. Consider how members of the military are generally prepared to risk their lives in a spirit of providing service to their country and its citizens.

■ Professionalism is similar, in the sense that it is commonly the case that members of particular professional groups feel strongly connected to their profession. For example, architects can feel that they are not just offering a service to the construction industry, but also collectively playing a part in creating attractive, functional and enjoyable urban and rural environments. In this way, professionalism includes a strong element of a higher calling, something above and beyond the intrinsic satisfactions and rewards of the work carried out.

■ Education and knowledge development activities are also closely associated with connectedness. People involved in teaching, training and research will commonly have a strong sense that they are not just earning a living, but also actively participating in a higher order venture of building, disseminat-ing and making use of knowledge that can be of value and make a positive difference. Being involved in the growth and development of another per-son and/or developing useful new knowledge amounts to more than just a job and so tends to be associated with a sense of higher purpose (and thus connectedness).

■ Science and technology bring people together in shared endeavour to explore the natural world and push back the boundaries of human knowledge.

■ Parenting is another very common source of connectedness, generally creat-ing a strong sense of playing a part in doing something very important for society and indeed for humanity. This is partly why parents will so often make personal sacrifices for the sake of their children. In addition, parents will often have a strong sense of connectedness to other parents.

■ Charitable causes of various kinds also have a tendency to generate a sense of connectedness, in terms of both connecting with like-minded fellow sup-porters of the specific cause, but also in the knowledge that a higher humani-tarian purpose is being served.

We need to bear in mind that these are in addition to religious forms of connectedness and will often overlap with them (for example, in terms of charity work and humanitarian causes more broadly).

All these possibilities complement and extend the earlier discussion of identity, meaning and purpose, and this is a major part of what makes connectedness so significant in relation to spirituality.

Promoting connectedness

Given the power and potential of connectedness, there is clearly much to be gained for people professionals to explore and capitalize on, promoting connectedness, whether through community-based opportunities to boost social capital or more individualized efforts to help people develop a sense of being part of something bigger than themselves.

Without a strong feeling of connectedness, the result can be a profound sense of alienation, of not belonging or not being valued as a human being (Jaeggi, 2016). This, in turn, can be an important factor in a number of social problems, such as drug misuse or other addiction-related problems.

Exercise 5

What problems in people's lives would you associate with a lack of connectedness? What options might there be for helping them to tackle such problems?

CHAPTER 6

Transcendence

Introduction

Literally, to transcend means to go beyond. In a religious context, it relates to the divine – that is, what transcends the earthly and takes us to a higher realm or higher power. As with so many other aspects of spirituality, there is also a secular equivalent. On a day-to-day basis we will generally get engrossed with basic activities around staying alive, earning a living, enjoying a certain quality of life and so on. In so doing, it is very easy to lose sight of the wider and deeper picture of human existence. Transcendence, in this non-religious sense, is therefore about going beyond everyday concerns and engaging with wider and deeper concerns about what it means to be human and how we can make the most of what human experience offers us.

Beyond the mundane

Canda et al. (2020) define transcendence as: 'experiences and interpretations of events as profound, breaking through banality and limitedness by time and space' (p. 96). This captures nicely the idea of going beyond the mundane. Consider the following scenarios:

■ Lee was so busy earning a living to feed his family that he spent very little time with his children and took being a parent for granted. However, when his eight-year-old daughter was involved in an accident and rushed into hospital, he had a transcendent moment. He remembered how miraculous it had been when he became a father and how much joy it filled him with. Being concerned that he might now lose his daughter made him acutely aware that he had allowed himself to get bogged down in the demands of everyday life

DOI: 10.4324/9781003682318-8

and had failed to appreciate the wonder of being a parent. He vowed that he would pay far more attention now to his role as a father.

- Susheela was diagnosed with breast cancer which led to several months of invasive treatments. Twelve months later she was told that her mammogram had shown the cancer had been completely removed, although she knew there would always be a danger it would come back. Looking back over the past year, she realized how the experience had been extremely trying, but she also acknowledged that it had made her much more appreciative of life and her otherwise good health.

- Adam had been brought up as an only child in an affluent family. As preparation for applying for a university place, he engaged in some voluntary work with a local community charity. This brought him into contact with families who were living in dire poverty in slum conditions and with a raft of problems to contend with. He was heartbroken to see, for example, children having to grow up in such adverse circumstances. It made him realize how privileged his upbringing had been and how sheltered he had been from some of the harsh realities of life. The experience gave him a much broader and deeper perspective on life.

Transcendence fits well with the idea of the numinous, as discussed earlier, that brings a sense of awe and wonder that takes us beyond the mundane and serves to make us more appreciative and therefore more spiritually enriched.

Key point

One very important aspect of transcendence is the recognition that the modern overemphasis on materialism serves as a barrier to spiritual growth and fulfilment. If people struggle to rise above materialistic concerns, then their chances of finding happiness and improving their wellbeing are likely to be severely limited.

Self-transcendence

Nietzsche wrote about the importance of what he called 'self-overcoming' (Nietzsche, 1998). His philosophy was based in part on the idea that humankind could be understood in terms of a rope that stretches from, at the lower extreme, our basic animal natures that make us part of 'the horde', to the peak of human achievement, the Ubermensch (generally translated as superman or overman, but actually gender neutral in its German original). Self-overcoming involves rising above our basic animal nature and aiming for a much higher level of human functioning and achievement. As such, it can be understood as a form of transcendence, specifically self-transcendence.

This fits well with the concept of self-empowerment and the long tradition of personal growth and development, a topic we shall revisit later.

Social transcendence

Davies (2014) offers an interesting perspective, based on Durkheim's work on religion:

> In his classic book, *The Elementary Forms of Religious Life,* Emile Durkheim (1912) developed the ideas of W. R. Smith on ancient sacrifice, arguing that communal rites integrated individuals within a unified community, including ancestors and deities, conferring a strength that elevated individuals above themselves. What people saw as God was, in Durkheim's view, a sense of society itself, and hence, for Durkheim, was understood as the ritual worship of society and the values and institutions it cherished.
>
> (p. 373)

'A strength that elevated individuals above themselves' tells us that we are talking about transcendence here. The idea of integrating 'individuals within a unified community' introduces the idea of social transcendence. That is, it is not simply a matter of *individual* transcendence; there is also the potential for community or social transcendence. This is commonly associated with disaster situations, catastrophes that have the effect of bringing people together in common cause – the Hillsborough disaster where almost 100 people were killed as a result of a failure of crowd management at a football match, for example. The ensuing vilification by the gutter press of the fans affected and the denial of responsibility by the authorities strengthened the shared sense of injustice and thus of connectedness and transcendence (Scraton, 2016).

But, it is not just at such times that communities or whole societies can engage in social transcendence, as a wide range of potential events can trigger at least some degree of *collective* transcendence where people rise above the mundane (elections, pandemics, major sporting events, terrorist attacks and so on).

Compassion

Earlier we mentioned compassion as a core value. We can also see it as being closely associated with transcendence in two ways. First, experiencing compassion can be the starting point for transcendence (at an individual level as in the case of Adam described above and collectively as in the case of, say, a mass shooting). Second, transcendence can be a spur to compassion – for example, when, by rising above the mundane and appreciating the world and our place within it at a higher level, we are moved to making the world a safer and more humane place.

Transcendence, then, is an important part of spirituality, whether channelled through faith or through humanitarian concern.

Exercise 6

How might you use the notion of transcendence in your work to make a positive difference to people's lives? What might this look like in concrete terms?

CHAPTER 7

Wisdom

Introduction

Having worked our way through the IMPACT framework, we now begin our exploration of the WINDOWS framework that complements and extends it. WINDOWS is an apt acronym, as spirituality is very much about how we look out upon the world. We begin by focusing on the significance of wisdom.

If we return to our working definition of spirituality as how we give expression to our chosen worldview, we can begin to see how wisdom fits into that picture. We are constantly having our senses exposed to information and processing it through our normal 'filters', the lenses we were taught through socialization as part of our upbringing. Beyond the immediate situation, we reject most of that information, retaining mainly only that which is of particular interest or value to us. In this way, we develop a knowledge base that in part defines who we are (taking us back to the importance of identity).

However, while knowledge and wisdom are closely related, they are not the same. We are sure that you have come across people who have a significant knowledge base, but who are unlikely to ever be described as wise. Wisdom goes well beyond knowledge. In a way, it can be understood as a skill or set of skills in the form of not just having knowledge, but also being able to use it effectively.

As we now enter an age characterized by the growing influence of artificial intelligence (AI), the growth of information (and easier access to it) can be seen as a blessing, but it also has its drawbacks, in the sense that relying on computer-generated knowledge has the potential to form an even greater disconnect between knowledge and information on the one hand and wisdom on the other.

DOI: 10.4324/9781003682318-9

Spiritual wisdom

What is of particular interest to us for present purposes is the notion of *spiritual* wisdom. This begins with spiritual awareness. People who adopt a 'head down, get on with it' approach to their life and rarely if ever consider wider or deeper issues are unlikely to achieve what could be called spiritual wisdom. The awareness we are talking about is often referred to as 'spiritual enlightenment' and is accompanied by a vast industry of pills, potions, programmes and paraphernalia, much of it resembling modern-day snake oil.

However, despite this commercialism, the idea of spiritual awareness as a basis for wisdom is an important one. A significant related concept is that of 'spiritual intelligence' (Zohar and Marshall, 2000). If we understand intelligence to be the ability to learn, then we can think of spiritual intelligence as the ability to learn in spiritually significant ways and thus serve as the basis of spiritual wisdom. Zohar and Marshall bemoan the common lack of such intelligence in what they call our 'spiritually dumb culture'.

Gardner (2006) puts forward a model of 'multiple intelligences', arguing that the conventional view of intelligence is too restrictive and does not take account of other forms of intelligence, such as musical or interpersonal. Vaughan (2002) links this notion with spiritual intelligence:

> This inquiry into spiritual intelligence suggests that it is one of several types of intelligence and that it can be developed relatively independently. Spiritual intelligence calls for multiple ways of knowing and for the integration of the inner life of mind and spirit with the outer life of work in the world. It can be cultivated through questing, inquiry, and practice.
>
> (p. 16)

Gardner did not use the term 'spiritual intelligence' itself, but he did include existential intelligence, by which he meant the ability to ponder such issues as the meaning of life and death. This is clearly consistent with the idea of spiritual intelligence and thus spiritual wisdom.

Spiritual capital

In a later work, Zohar and Marshall go on to link spiritual intelligence to 'spiritual capital'. Influenced by the work of Bourdieu (2021) who wrote about social capital (the network of valuable social contacts we can have) and cultural capital (access to cultural resources – for example, through education and engagement in cultural activities such as the arts), they describe spiritual capital as:

> wealth that we can live by, wealth that enriches the deeper aspects of our lives. It is wealth we gain through drawing upon our deepest meanings,

deepest values, most fundamental purposes, and highest motivations, and by finding a way to embed these in our lives and work.

(2004, p. 3)

The parallel between economic wealth in a materialistically driven culture and spiritual wealth echoes the common concern that the modern world has lost touch with what is important in life and become fixated with money and materialism. It is as if there is a counterbalance: the more a society focuses on economic wealth, the less it focuses on building spiritual capital and thus the less spiritual wisdom there is to be drawn on.

Reflective moment

Are you satisfied with your own level of spiritual capital? If not, what opportunities might you be able to capitalize on to build it up?

Wisdom as wrestling with complexity

Kierkegaard, as we noted earlier, was critical of approaches to religion that promoted faith as simply following a pattern dictated by others and emphasized the need to find authenticity by each person finding their own way forward. As Armstrong (1993) explains:

> The Danish philosopher Søren Kierkegaard (1813–55) insisted that the old creeds and doctrines had become idols, ends in and substitutes for the ineffable reality of God. True Christian faith was a leap out of the world, away from these fossilised human beliefs and outmoded attitudes, into the unknown.

(p. 415)

This reflects a longstanding tension between an externally imposed set of behavioural norms and the onus on the individual to make their own decisions. It raises the key question of: Is moral responsibility a matter of complying with edicts or making ethical choices based on our own judgement?

For many people who reject religion, a significant part of their rationale for doing so is precisely a rejection of, in effect, being told what to do and what to believe. For many people of faith, it is the sense of certainty that such edicts give rise to that appeals to them (we shall return to this point below when we discuss the role of security).

But this is not simply a tension between believers and non-believers. The same tension arises within religions (as is the case for Kierkegaard's approach to Christianity) and between religions. In terms of the latter, one of the meanings of Islam is 'submission' (to the will of God), while Buddhism has no concept of a deity and Taoism emphasizes the need for each person to follow 'the Way', but not in a prescribed fashion (balancing the yin of firmness with the yang of flexibility – Cleary, 2003).

Wrestling with these complications is partly what spiritual wisdom is all about. It involves recognizing that spirituality, whether religion based or not, presents challenges, dilemmas and a potentially bumpy road. Spiritual wisdom is both what can guide us on that road and what we can learn from the journey.

Key point

Spiritual wisdom is not about 'right answers'; it is about using our spiritual intelligence to make sense of our lives and helping others to make sense of theirs in a context of competing perspectives and powerful vested interests on the part of established groups and networks.

Exercise 7

What options are available for helping people to develop spiritual wisdom, whether within or outside a religious context? What obstacles might there be to developing such wisdom, and what can be done to remove or bypass them?

CHAPTER 8

Integrity

Introduction

Integrity, in the sense we are using it here, refers to living consistently with one's values. It is unfortunately the case that many people profess a set of values, but do not necessarily abide by them in their day-to-day interactions – for example, someone who claims to be committed to equality and fairness but who none the less treats people unfairly at times. Integrity, then, is about values and the ability or willingness to live and act consistently with them.

In an earlier work (Thompson and Moss, 2026), we argued that values are key to safe, ethical and effective practice across the people professions. If we disregard the beliefs and principles that we are committed to, then we run the risk that our practice can do more harm than good. For example, in working with people who are commonly discriminated against, if we fail to take account of the significance of equality, diversity and inclusion as value positions, we risk adding to their experiences of oppression. Rather than playing a part in empowering them to enhance their wellbeing, we could actually be decreasing it.

The source of values

For many people, there is only one recognized source of values and that is religion. It is assumed that anyone who follows an atheistic path is therefore not in a position to live an ethical, values-driven life. Of course, this is far from the truth, as the Dalai Lama (2011) has shown, as have innumerable examples of strongly ethical practices that have no connection with any religious beliefs or practices.

Interestingly, Richard Holloway, the bishop who lost his faith, but nonetheless retained a strong sense of spirituality that we mentioned earlier,

   DOI: 10.4324/9781003682318-10

goes so far as to argue that values and meanings are of human, not divine, construction:

> We may be no closer to understanding why there is a world, but we are now able to accept the fact that the world itself is the source of the values and meanings we prize most, not some hypothetical transcendent reality which did none of the work yet claims all the credit. One way to express this is to say that the spirit is now engendered by and encountered in the world in which we find ourselves. Rather than positing an external force to account for our most cherished experiences, we begin to understand how they were generated within us in response to the life process itself.
>
> (2005, p. 31)

So, whether we see values as emanating from a divine or human source, our challenge is to be aware of them and the problems that arise when practice is not values based.

> **TIP!** It helps to be clear what your own values are, to make them explicit. This puts you in a stronger position when it comes to ensuring that you practise with integrity. Being aware of what other people's values are can also be useful for casting light on complex situations.

Obstacles to integrity

There are various reasons why at times integrity can be lacking, not least the following:

- There is no real commitment to the professed values. The person concerned is just making what they see as suitable noises to give the impression that their work is based on appropriate professional values. For example, someone who harbours racist beliefs may express a commitment to anti-discriminatory practice in order to avoid criticism, censure or even disciplinary action.
- There is a lack of awareness of the disconnect. For example, someone who is genuinely committed to anti-sexism may not realize that they are behaving in a sexist way, as they do not recognize that they are relying on one or more sexist stereotypes that were part of the culture they were brought up in. Similarly, people may not appreciate that certain forms of language they commonly use have discriminatory connotations.
- At times, people will be so busy that they are rushing to get the job done and, in their haste, have lost sight of their values and their importance. For example, confidentiality may be breached when an overpressurized worker passes

on information unthinkingly, having not considered the consequences of doing so.

- An individual's emotional state can also stand in the way of acting with integrity. Someone who is angry, upset, afraid or deeply frustrated may well, in the spur of the moment, treat others in a less than dignified way, a way that they would not normally adopt.
- There can also be organizational factors, such as a lack of suitable relevant training on the key issues and/or an organizational culture that negates the values – for example, a culture characterized by negativity and cynicism.

The full list of obstacles would be very long indeed and would include such matters as censorship, coercion, conformity and a lack of cultural competence. Being aware of these obstacles can help us avoid them or circumnavigate them, while also alerting us to the potential for each of these in others.

Values and compassion

We have already drawn on the helpful work of the Dalai Lama and once again he offers a helpful perspective when he argues that: 'The essence of compassion is a desire to alleviate the suffering of others and to promote their well-being. This is the spiritual principle from which all other positive inner values emerge' (2013, p. xi).

Later we shall discuss how religion has achieved both compassionate and destructive outcomes in various ways. But, for now, we want to acknowledge that compassion (and associated values) is a common theme across religions. Again, though, we need to recognize that compassion is not limited to people of faith. Humanistic endeavours are also strongly rooted in a commitment to compassion.

What we need to be aware of, then, is that compassion is at the heart of integrity, in the sense that integrity without compassion is of little value in terms of the work of people professionals in supporting, protecting and empowering the people who rely on what we have to offer and compassion without integrity amounts to little more than what today would be called 'virtue signalling' (trying to impress people with our expressed concern, rather than focusing on making a positive difference).

Exercise 8

How might you recognize a lack of integrity in others (that is, a gap between their value statements and their actions)? What options might be available to you in order to address such a gap with a view to preventing or reducing the problems associated with a lack of integrity?

CHAPTER 9

Nurturance

Introduction

No (wo)man is an island; we are all interconnected through society. While individualism is a strong feature of western thinking, it is none the less the case that we cannot be separated from our social context (Thompson, 2018a). This has many implications, but the one we are particularly interested in is the complex sets of interpersonal dynamics that can make such an important difference to our wellbeing and our lives more broadly. In straightforward terms, when we interact with another person, we can enrich their life or diminish it (depending on how we act towards them) and, of course, how they act towards us can enrich or diminish our lives. Nurturance is about making sure that, as far as possible, we are focusing on the enrichment and avoiding the diminishment.

Buber's I-Thou and I-it

The work of Martin Buber has proven to be very influential in various places. In particular, his distinction between I-Thou and I-it has proven helpful (Buber, 1958). I-Thou refers to interactions that involve mutual respect and which are therefore enriching to both parties; they are interactions where both parties engage fully in the process of communication. I-it interactions are, by contrast, purely instrumental; they are just about 'getting the job done'. While they may well get the job done, they are likely to diminish both parties, as no genuine human connection has taken place.

I-Thou generally involves a degree of warmth, accompanied by active listening and a genuine willingness to make the interaction productive. I-it interactions are basically stripped down to the bare essentials of what needs to be done.

DOI: 10.4324/9781003682318-11

Buber's work raises the question of whether our interactions are empowering and enriching or disempowering and diminishing. This highlights just how important interactions are. They can be positive and nurturing or negative and undermining.

TIP! In seeking to ensure our interactions are I-Thou, rather than I-it, we need to remember that nonverbal communication has a vitally important role to play. It can help or hinder in significant ways.

The human connection

Thompson (2018b) emphasizes the spiritual enrichment to be gained from human connection in stating that:

> we must never lose sight of the fact that the people we are serving are human beings (with all that this entails), nor too must we lose sight of the fact that we are human (with all that that entails).
>
> (p. 137)

Things can go sadly (and sometimes tragically) adrift if we do not pay heed to this important message. Treating people in a way that denies or disrespects their humanity is likely to be ineffective and could potentially do a lot of harm (wreck someone's confidence, for example). Forgetting our own humanity (in neglecting self-care, for example) can also be highly problematic in terms of stress, sickness absence and so on.

The renowned existentialist thinker Jean-Paul Sartre is famous for, amongst other things, arguing that 'hell is other people' (Sartre, 1989). By this he meant that other people's plans regularly get in the way of our own plans. Consider these brief examples:

- The ideal job for Jaswinder is advertised and he becomes excited by the prospect of being successful in applying for it. However, he is not even shortlisted as so many other highly qualified and experienced people apply for it too.
- Anne is in a hurry to catch the train, but heavy traffic leaves her little time to park the car and, when she finds that the station car park is full, by the time she finds alternative parking she has missed the train.
- Keith wants to book a table at his wife's favourite restaurant to celebrate their wedding anniversary, but the date coincides with a local festival, which means that the restaurant (and most of the others in town) are fully booked.

These are examples where no one is necessarily trying to cause us problems, but it is just that what they are trying to do (their 'projects', to use Sartre's term) is causing us problems in terms of our own projects.

However, what Sartre did not acknowledge is that other people can be heaven too, in the sense that the nurturance of others can be immensely empowering, affirming and validating and thus tremendously supportive (another example of connected-ness). This can especially be the case when we are in need of comfort and solace, such as when we are grieving or feeling very vulnerable for whatever reason.

This is where nurturance comes clearly into the picture for those situations requiring compassion and a genuine sense of human-to-human connection. Adopting a stance of nurturance is not difficult, but it can be immensely powerful and positive.

TIP! Be careful not to underestimate the power of reassurance. Self-doubt is a very common phenomenon that can cause significant problems for many people. Offering a degree of (realistic) reassurance can make a huge difference. By 'realistic' we mean avoiding giving false hopes or setting people up to fail.

Love

The concept of love is a very complex one (Illouz, 2012). There are, of course, different types of love (romantic love vs. parental love, for example), but, what-ever the type of love, we would see nurturance as an important part of it. How-ever, it does not follow that you need to love someone to offer nurturance. For example, social workers do not need to love their clients, health care workers do not need to love their patients and managers do not need to love their staff. But, if each of these people professionals wants to achieve optimal outcomes, then a focus on nurturance is very much in order.

Key point

When people interact, they can enrich or diminish one another, and so the out-comes can be positive or negative. Recognizing nurturance as an important feature of human spirituality can help us to focus on making sure that, for our own part, we are doing whatever we reasonably can to make the interactions (and the rela-tionships that grow from them) positive, empowering, enriching and nurturing.

Exercise 9

Think of two or more people you regard as very good at nurturing others, peo-ple who, just through their interaction skills, are able to enrich other people's life experiences. Think now of two or more people whose interactions with others tend to be problematic and undermining. What do you see as the key differences between the positive interactions and the negative ones? What can you learn from this?

CHAPTER 10

Direction

Introduction

In our earlier discussions of meaning and purpose we made reference to the value of having a sense of direction. Here we explore the implications of that in a little more detail.

'Empty life syndrome' is a term used to refer to people who lack any sense of purpose or direction in their lives. It is often associated with materialism and a lack of spiritual awareness, a life stuck in the mud of the mundane. A common example would be parents who have focused heavily on their children as a source of meaning, purpose and satisfaction who then feel spiritually empty when their children grow up and leave home. Direction, in the spiritual sense is, in many ways the proposed antidote to empty life syndrome, regardless of how it has arisen.

In this chapter we discuss three important ideas relating to direction – the existentialist conception of life as a journey, a horizontal approach to career development and the currently highly popular notion of mindfulness.

Life as a journey

We are not fixed entities; we move, grow and develop through our lives (Green, 2010). We therefore have hopes and aspirations, visions of the future we want to create. For some people, this is characterized by a strong sense of direction, a carefully worked out plan of action; for others, they have a broad sense of direction, but no clear plan to bring about their desired ends; while yet others have relatively little sense of direction and prefer to take each day as it comes.

The commonsense idea that we have a relatively fixed personality that is on a journey through life does not fit with the reality of human experience which is

DOI: 10.4324/9781003682318-12

characterized by constant change and the ever-present potential for growth and development. A more accurate picture is that we are that journey – our life is that process; we are constantly 'becoming'.

This presents us with choices about how we manage that journey. Do we opt for a preplanned, predetermined itinerary, as is the case for many members of faith communities where there are sacred texts that do not offer a precise, detailed itinerary but do map out an overall route as to how life should be lived. Other religious traditions, especially eastern ones, tend to be more general and less prescriptive in their approach to life direction.

However, it is not simply about religious diversity. Secular approaches to direction also vary considerably. For example, there is a strong tradition of promoting goal setting as a worthwhile approach to self-management, while the more recent emphasis on mindfulness places far more emphasis on savouring the present moment. Perhaps the wise way forward is to find a balance between some degree of future orientation, which is what goal setting is all about, while not losing sight of the value of being 'present in the moment' (we shall return to this point below).

Horizontal career development

Thompson and McGowan (2024) discuss an important distinction between vertical and horizontal career development. The former refers to the traditional idea of upward mobility over time through one or more promotions. The latter, by contrast, is where employees seek a sense of fulfilment not through rising through the ranks, but through engaging in developmental activities, such as: supervising or mentoring less experienced staff or students; contributing to education and training; engaging in developmental schemes and programmes, and so on.

Sadly, many people think narrowly in terms of vertical career development (and the associated 'rat race' problems) and remain unaware of the benefits of gaining a sense of direction horizontally, rather than vertically. Helping people to explore such opportunities can open important doors in many circumstances and is therefore an important issue to consider.

Reflective moment

What opportunities for horizontal career development do you have available to you? What activities can you engage in that will help give a sense of direction and fulfilment without necessarily involving promotion efforts?

Mindfulness and the eternal present

We have already made reference to the popularity of mindfulness. The basic idea behind it is that modern life has a tendency to overload us and fill our heads with all sorts of thoughts and feelings, and this overload can prevent us from appreciating the specialness of every moment and thereby leave us disempowered and spiritually diminished (the emergence of AI can be seen to intensify this problem).

It is not surprising, then, that the idea of replacing a full mind with a mindful approach has so much appeal. Being mindful involves focusing on the present moment. This does not mean that we should abandon any sense of direction, but, rather, it is about not allowing the busyness of life to overcrowd us.

Death awareness

Of course, it would be a serious omission to discuss direction as a spiritual phenomenon without discussing death, in the sense that death is the direction we are all heading in! Sadly, treating death as a taboo topic is a common phenomenon, even though being aware of our own mortality (and therefore appreciating the limited time we have on Earth) is arguably a highly spiritually enriching approach to the finite nature of our existence.

While the idea that we should live each day as if it were our last is hardly feasible in any concrete sense, there is certainly much to be gained from avoiding living the lie of assuming that death is something that happens only to other people.

Exercise 10

What benefits do you associate with having a balanced sense of direction and what problems do you envisage arising from too strong an emphasis on such a sense of direction (focusing so much on the future that we lose sight of the present)?

CHAPTER 11

Openness to experience and learning

Introduction

Life experience is something that even hermits cannot avoid. This topic therefore raises some important issues that are worth exploring.

Broadening our horizons

Openness to experience varies significantly. At one extreme, many people limit their experiences quite significantly – for example, as a result of anxiety or perhaps due to one or more adverse experiences that have led them to be very cautious about what situations they expose themselves to. At the other extreme, we have people who seek to maximize their range of experiences and broaden their horizons as fully as they can. Classically, this spectrum is represented by the tension between Apollo who represents order and Dionysus who represents adventure.

While each extreme can be seen as potentially problematic and dangerous, finding a suitable balance can be a spiritually significant step.

Reflective moment

Where are you on this spectrum? Are you tending towards putting yourself at risk by not being sufficiently cautious in facing risky situations or are you perhaps spiritually diminished by being overly cautious and denying yourself potentially life-enhancing and enriching experiences?

DOI: 10.4324/9781003682318-13

Instrumental learning vs. growth

When it comes to learning from our experience, we need to acknowledge that such learning does not happen automatically. Many people have had significant experiences but learnt little or nothing from them. Experience offers the raw materials for learning, but we have to make the learning happen if we are to get the benefit of what our experience can teach us.

Many people lose out because they either do not appreciate that the experience is not enough on its own or there are reasons why they do not take the learning process forward, possibly due to anxiety, having had bad experiences of learning (a bullying, confidence-wrecking teacher, for example) or some other such reason.

Helping people to become more effective learners can therefore be a positive contribution to enhanced spirituality. This is especially the case when learning goes beyond an instrumental approach to one focused on personal growth. What we mean by an instrumental approach is one where the learning is narrow, specific and task focused, ranging from learning how to tie your shoelaces to learning how to fly a supersonic jet. Such learning is important, but it is no substitute for personal growth, by which we mean learning that not only develops knowledge or skills, but it also helps us to develop as people (what is often referred to as 'existential learning'). It is in this sense that personal growth can be seen as spiritual, as something that affects who we are, our sense of purpose and direction and so on. It can contribute also to our sense of awe and wonder as well as to our connectedness.

Personal vs professional development

Personal growth and development can, of course, apply to anyone at any time. However, by professional development, we mean learning and growth in terms of profession-specific knowledge, skills and especially values. The former contributes very much to the latter but is not enough on its own. To produce the best results, there has to also be learning relating to the specifics of the profession concerned.

However, we should note that professional development can also contribute to personal growth. For example, the pride we can take in the important work we do in our profession can boost our confidence while also contributing to the benefits we gain from the sense of connectedness that professionalism brings.

Finding the growth zone

Thompson (2024a) discusses the importance of the growth zone, the healthy balance in terms of fostering learning that lies between the complacency of the comfort zone and learning-inhibiting effects of the danger zone (Figure 11.1).

For optimal learning to take place, people need to feel reasonably comfortable and safe (so that they are not distracted by a sense of threat), but not so safe and

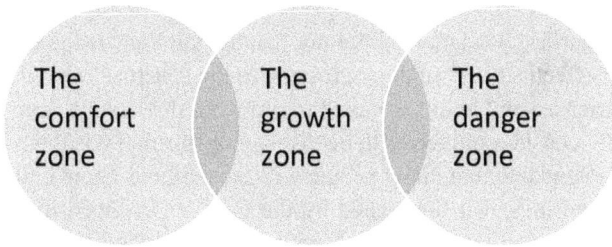

Figure 11.1 Finding the growth zone

comfortable that they are not motivated to learn or make any changes. Finding the growth zone balance can be difficult at times, but worth the effort.

Self-directed learning

The way the education system works tends to create and reinforce the view that learning is a passive process; it is something that is largely done *to* people. It is learning professionals, rather than learners, who tend to make the decisions about is learned, how it is learned and where it is learned (by setting the curriculum, for example). However, self-directed learning (heutagogy, to use the technical term) is increasingly being recognized as a more effective way of optimizing learning (Thompson, 2024a). This involves the learner being in the driving seat for their own learning journey, taking a more proactive approach to deciding what they need to learn and how best they can learn it (with the appropriate support, as required – self-directed learning does not need to be carried out alone).

Self-directed learning can therefore be seen as having a spiritual dimension, in so far as it fits well with such concepts as identity, meaning, purpose and direction.

Humility

You can't please all the people all the time; there will always be limitations in terms of what we can achieve in any given situation. This is where humility comes into the picture. We need to accept that there will be times when we get things wrong, when we fail or we don't meet (our own) expectations. Being humble means that we come to terms with this and do not beat ourselves up over being less than perfect.

Making the mistake of assuming that less than perfect means less than adequate will limit our learning and discourage us from being open to new experiences where there is a risk of failure. We need to remember that failure is not the opposite of success, it is part of the process of success. Great scientists have achieved success not by avoiding failure, but by learning from the experience of failure and thereby making progress.

Spiritual wisdom

As we noted earlier, wisdom is about not just having knowledge but also being able to use it effectively. If we do not recognize the spiritual value of being open to new experiences and being prepared to draw out the lessons from them, then we can hardly consider ourselves to be displaying spiritual wisdom.

It is understandable that many people will feel anxious about embracing new experiences and may feel threatened by the changes involved in learning and growth. However, it also needs to be understood that there is a high personal price to pay for allowing such anxiety to dominate and hold us back from getting the best out of our lives.

Exercise 11

List as many reasons as you can think of as to why people may be reluctant to engage in new experiences and/or draw out the learning from their experiences. For each one think of possible ways of removing or minimizing these obstacles.

CHAPTER 12

Wellbeing

Introduction

Just being alive is, of course, something to be thankful for, but it is generally reasonable to expect more than that, to expect a certain quality of life, and that quality of life is precisely what we mean by wellbeing. Although many people in many circumstances will have little or no quality of life, we will tend to view such situations in terms of there being something wrong. That is, the idea that we should have some degree of wellbeing has come to be expected – more of a right than a privilege. As Foley (2011) comments: 'So we are not only born to strive, but to strive for *well-being*' (p. 63).

Dimensions of wellbeing

Thompson (2019a) writes about being WISE about wellbeing, with WISE spelling out:

- *Workplace wellbeing* Work is a major part of most people's lives, and so our experiences in the workplace will have a significant bearing on our quality of life.
- *Individual wellbeing* This is linked to health, but also separate from it. It is possible to be healthy, but with a very poor quality of life or to be in poor health, yet still manage to have a good quality of life.
- *Social wellbeing* Quality of life depends a great deal on 'social location' – that is, where we are situated in terms of class, ethnic group, gender and so on. What happens at a societal level is therefore important in terms of people's wellbeing.

DOI: 10.4324/9781003682318-14

Figure 12.1 Types of wellbeing

■ *Environmental wellbeing* Destruction of our habitat and the pressing need to halt the damage is clearly a key issue when it comes to wellbeing.

It may surprise you that spiritual wellbeing is not included in this typology. This is because, in a very real sense, all aspects of wellbeing are spiritual, in so far as they relate to how we give expression to our chosen worldview. They are fundamental aspects of how we live our lives (Figure 12.1).

The social context

The literature on wellbeing tends to be predominantly individualistic but, as we mentioned a moment ago, the social context is highly important. For example, people who are exposed to discrimination and oppression are likely to face additional barriers when it comes to establishing and maintaining a high quality of life.

One particularly significant factor in this regard is 'alienation' – the feeling of not being accepted or welcome, of being 'other', of not belonging. It arises in many ways, mainly where social processes, institutions and discourses combine to give a subtle (and sometimes not so subtle) message to the effect that certain people are not as valued as others, as alien or 'not like us'.

This includes people who experience mental health problems where alienation is commonly a significant feature (Thompson, 2019b) and also to a certain extent to people with disabilities where failures to address their specific needs gives a strong message of exclusion. As the social model of disability makes clear, the process of *dis*abling is social – it is to do with social attitudes towards disability, restrictive policies, failure to invest in reasonable adjustments and so on (Barnes and Mercer, 2010).

In a sense, alienation represents a degree of spiritual impoverishment, a barrier to spiritual wellbeing. We need to understand it not simply as a subjective feeling, but as a reflection of broader social factors that create significant inequalities in terms of access to wellbeing.

> **TIP!** The significance of alienation is often neglected by people professionals in trying to make sense of situations they are involvedwith (the process of assessment, for example). Including a consideration of the role of alienation in people's lives can therefore enrich our understanding and make us more effective in our work.

Stress as an obstacle to wellbeing

The traditional approach to stress is primarily individualistic – that is, stress is commonly seen as a person's failure to be able to manage their pressures effectively. This has a tendency to pathologize the individual concerned by failing to take account of wider social and organizational factors (Thompson, 2024b). This creates a danger of vicious circles developing: a person becomes stressed and needs support, but they do not ask for support for fear of being labelled as weak or 'a poor coper'; without support they become more stressed; the more stressed they are, the more reluctant they are to ask for support for fear of being stigmatized. And so it goes on.

It is therefore important to recognize that, while stress is a significant concern for individuals, it is very much a social and organizational phenomenon. Consider, for example, how organizational factors like work overload, bullying, poor leadership and inadequate support can contribute to stress, while social factors like the misuse or abuse of power, sexism, stigmatization, poverty and so on are also often significant factors.

So, when we are considering wellbeing – especially spiritual wellbeing – we need to bear stress and mind and not reduce it to a set of individual factors when these wider issues are so significant.

The importance of work

We mentioned earlier the importance of work in most people's lives and how significant changes in the world of work have added significant pressures for a wide range of people. Jaffe (2021) writes at length about the negative aspects of working life, and it is certainly the case that work expectations have grown significantly over time in many areas of society. As Jaffe points out, demands have tended to increase, while associated rewards have not. Working life therefore has considerable potential to stand in the way of wellbeing and happiness (Bevan and Cooper, 2022; Burchell, 2023).

However, work can also be a significant source of wellbeing and be immensely rewarding in spiritual terms (consider, for example, the negative impact in terms of spiritual impoverishment brought about by unemployment). Indeed, when it comes to wellbeing, the workplace and how it is managed can make all the difference.

If we want to enhance wellbeing and promote spiritual enrichment, then we need – individually, collectively and societally – to make sure that we are giving due consideration to workplace issues (hence the importance of trade unionism).

Exercise 12

In what ways is wellbeing affected by social factors? What possibilities exist to influence such factors?

CHAPTER 13

Security

Introduction

There are different types of security, not least physical, emotional and ontological. Physical security is about feeling relatively safe from attack or physical
harm. Emotional security is about feeling able to deal with the emotional ups and
downs of life. Ontological security is more complex. It is about feeling safe and
comfortable with who we are ('in our own skin', as it is often put) and therefore
closely related to the idea of identity. Arguably, there are spiritual aspects to all
forms of security, but we want to focus here on ontological (or existential) security in particular, as we regard it as being particularly significant when it comes
to spirituality.

Ontological security

Our sense of security can be general or specific. Imagine, for example, being
in a bar when a fight breaks out. Prior to this you may have felt quite physically
safe and secure, but now you suddenly start fearing that you may get caught up
in the violence, and so you feel physically at risk in a way you did not do before.
Your concerns are specific. However, in situations where you may have been
traumatized, you may well generalize your insecurity to a range of situations.
For example, if you were involved in a serious road traffic accident, you may sub-
sequently find yourself feeling quite insecure whenever you are in a car or other
motor vehicle (for a while at least).

Ontological security works in the same way. For example, someone may feel
quite comfortable with who they are – they are 'at peace' with themselves – but,
after experiencing a major loss, they are likely to feel greatly disorientated and
'at sea'. It is not uncommon for people who are deep in the throes of grief to say

DOI: 10.4324/9781003682318-15

words to the effect of: 'I don't know who I am anymore'. However, such insecurities can make themselves felt more broadly, as in the case of people diagnosed with schizophrenia where retaining a coherent sense of self tends to prove very difficult (schizophrenia is better thought of as a 'shattered' personality than the inaccurate stereotype of a 'split' personality).

Ontological insecurity can therefore be a short-term phenomenon associated with specific circumstances or a longer-term challenge for certain individuals or groups of people. We can all experience ontological insecurity at times, but some people, for various reasons, are much more prone to it and therefore face more significant spiritual challenges because of it.

Sources of security

For a significant proportion of the population, religion is their primary source of security. As Hamilton (1995) explains:

> Religion provides compensation by presenting a picture of a world order in which everything has meaning, everything fits into place and nothing is arbitrary and accidental. All sins will be punished in the long run. Those who seem to prosper by wrongdoing will receive their punishment in due course. Their actions do not invalidate or undermine the moral order. Without this type of belief, Freud argues, the moral order would break down.
>
> (p. 68)

However, for others, this is not a solution, as Hitchens, one of the 'new atheists' we will discuss later, puts it: 'As for consolation, since religious people so often insist that faith answers this supposed need, I shall simply say that those who offer false consolation are false friends' (p. 9).

For those who reject religious sources of security, other ways of achieving at least a basic degree of security need to be found. Often, this will be through connectedness, as discussed earlier, in the sense of both being involved in something bigger than ourselves (political or humanitarian causes, for example) and having some amount of social capital to draw on (friends, relatives, organizational memberships and so on).

Culture itself can also be a source of security. The reassuring routines and well-established patterns that go to make up a culture contribute to a sense of identity, belonging and therefore security. Rituals, whether religious or otherwise, are an important part of this. Bowie (2007) describes a ritual as: 'in some sense a performance or cultural drama' (p. 145). She elaborates:

> Rituals have many functions, both at the level of the individual and for groups or societies. They can channel and express emotions, guide and reinforce forms of behaviour, support or subvert the status quo, bring about change, or restore harmony and balance. Rituals also have a very important

role in healing. They may be used to maintain the life forces and fertility of the earth, and to restore right relationships with the unforeseen world, whether of spirits, ancestors, deities, or other supernatural forces. The succession of a culture's most deeply held values from one generation to another may be facilitated by means of ritual. Rituals are also intimately connected with violence, destruction, and scapegoating. Above all, they are dramatic. Rituals can be seen as performances, which involve both audiences and actors.

(p. 138)

Culture also applies in the sense of culture in the form of the arts, music, literature and so on. The trappings of the familiar, especially trappings that bring us pleasure, play a large part in bolstering our sense of security.

Key point

Spiritual fulfilment is, of course, a source of security in its own right. The more spiritually nourished we feel, the more secure we are likely to feel (and vice versa – a potential virtuous circle).

Contingency and flux

These are terms widely used in the existentialist literature. Contingency refers to the lack of certainty in life, based on the recognition that life can change drastically at any moment (due to an accident or crime, for example). Flux refers to the fact that everything is steadily changing. We are growing older with every breath, physical objects are steadily deteriorating at a very slow pace, and so on.

The combination of these two factors means that we need to be aware that security, fixity and certainty are not a natural state – quite the opposite, in fact. So, the major implication of this is that security is not something we can take for granted; it is something we need to build. We each face the challenge of developing a reasonable sense of security for ourselves, with the support of others, of course. Likewise, it can be argued that we have a duty to help others develop and sustain a sense of security (hence the important role of nurturance as part of spirituality). This is clearly part of good parenting, for example, as well as a significant factor in leadership in the workplace and beyond.

From a practice point of view, it is essential to get the balance right. That is, assuming that everything is fixed and stable, including our own identity, will not prepare us or the people we are seeking to support, protect or empower for the changes that will inevitably come (this links with our earlier discussion of essentialism). By the same token, we do not want to go to the opposite extreme and feel overly anxious or overwhelmed by contingency and flux.

Once again, connectedness and nurturance can be important factors here. They can help to keep anxiety and anguish within manageable limits and help us to develop the confidence we need to rise to the challenges involved.

Exercise 13

Some people seem to have major problems establishing and maintaining a sense of security in their lives. What possible reasons might there be for this and what could possibly be done to help address such problems?

CHAPTER 14

Spirituality today and tomorrow

Introduction

In our view, spirituality has remained 'submerged' for far too long, especially in the people professions where being able to establish an authentic human connection is so essential as a basis for best practice. Now, thankfully, there is a growing interest in spirituality as a key feature of life in broad terms and, more narrowly, as an important consideration when working with people, their problems and their potential. This chapter highlights some key issues about spirituality in terms of our current and emerging understanding and seeks to form a basis for understanding for further development.

Spirituality beyond religion

For many people, spirituality is simply a subdivision of religion, and so, if we are not involved in religious matters for any reason, why should we pay attention to spirituality? There are, of course, two things wrong with this approach. First, as we shall be arguing later, we should be taking account of religious matters anyway where these are of importance to the individual, family or community concerned. For many people, religion is a major part of who they are and how they make sense of their lives, and so, in those situations where we need to have a good understanding of the people we are seeking to support, empower or protect, it could be a significant mistake to omit consideration of religion and what it means to the people concerned. We could also be ignoring potentially helpful sources of support and access to useful resources.

Second, as we have been at pains to point out, spirituality is something that applies to everyone, not just to members of faith communities. Spiritual needs

DOI: 10.4324/9781003682318-16

are human needs, and we all face spiritual challenges, whether we are religious or not. Indeed, so many of the problems people wrestle with are either spiritual in nature or have spiritual associations: dealing with loss and change; managing conflict and other relationship challenges; responding to abuse and trauma; addiction; maintaining a sense of purpose and direction; and so on. Trying to address what are often fundamentally spiritual matters without any knowledge, understanding or consideration of spirituality could be making situations substantially worse – that is, being part of the problem, rather than part of the solution.

In short, spirituality matters, and we neglect it at our peril.

Our own spirituality

Taking account of people's spiritual needs, challenges and resources is clearly an important basis for good practice (including management practice). However, that is not the whole story. We also have to include consideration of our own spirituality.

We made the point earlier that it is perfectly possible (and, indeed, common) for people to be religious but not spiritually fulfilled by their faith, while people of no faith can succeed in finding spiritual fulfilment without faith. It is therefore an oversimplification to assume that religion automatically provides spiritual satisfaction, and an absence of faith means an absence of spiritual satisfaction. As we have already begun to see, the relationship between religion and spirituality is complex and multidimensional.

So, if you are a person of faith, does your religion currently meet your spiritual needs or do you need to find other, supplementary ways of doing so? If you are not a person of faith, are you able to identify and meet your spiritual needs, or is there more you need to do to move forward in that regard?

An important issue in terms of our own spirituality is the significance of self-care. This is particularly relevant to the people professions, as the pressures of wrestling with the complexities of people's problems and potential can be immense and can do a great deal of harm if they are not well managed. The selflessness that brings so many people into the people professions is certainly a positive in terms of compassion and other values. However, it can also be a liability if it means that we neglect self-care and allow ourselves to become burnt out or so stressed that we are practising dangerously.

Effective self-care includes making sure that our own spiritual needs are being addressed properly. Sacrificing them for the sake of other people's needs may appear to be a virtuous thing to do, but it is a very unwise step to take.

Always make sure that you are not neglecting your own needs. You are not doing anybody any favours by placing your own health and well-being at risk. 'You can't pour from an empty vessel' is an adage that you should constantly bear in mind.

Shared spirituality

Tomikel (2010) states that: 'Spirituality is a personal solitary achievement. It is like the Buddhist idea of Nirvana. You don't take anyone with you on that journey' (p. 5). While we would agree that each person's spiritual challenges are unique to their own circumstances, the idea that spirituality has to be a solitary – rather than shared – activity is both inaccurate and unhelpful.

So much of what is important in spiritual terms is social in nature. Indeed, whatever aspect of spirituality we consider, it takes little effort to see that social factors are part of the picture. The idea that spirituality is a solitary pursuit is likely to lead us to look within for answers and potentially disregard the important spiritual strengths that come from human connection and community. Yes, looking within is part of it, but limiting ourselves to that amounts to failing to appreciate the vitally important *shared* nature of spirituality as a social phenomenon.

Spirituality and religion

In the next chapter, we shall switch our focus from spirituality to religion. So, as a form of 'bridge' between our discussions of spirituality so far and the discussions of religion to come, we return to the important work of Canda et al. (2020) who very helpfully highlight the key elements of both topics:

Spirituality Is …
A process of human life and development

- focusing on the search for a sense of meaning, purpose, morality, and well-being;
- in relationship with oneself, other people, other beings, the universe and ultimate reality however understood (e.g., in animistic, atheistic, nontheistic, polytheistic, or other ways);
- orienting around centrally significant priorities; and
- engaging a sense of transcendence (i.e., experience of what is deeply profound, sacred, or transpersonal).

(p. 96)

They go on to describe religion in the following terms:

Religion Is …
A systematic, and organized pattern of values, beliefs, symbols, behaviours and experiences that involves

- spirituality;
- a community of adherents;
- transmissions of traditions over time; and

- individual and community support functions (e.g., organizational structure, material assistance, emotional support, or political advocacy) that are directly or indirectly related to spirituality.

(pp. 97–8)

Of course, there is so much more that could be said about both of these phenomena, but we hope that the clarity offered by Canda et al. will help you make the connections between what we have said so far about spirituality and what we are about to say about religion.

Exercise 14

If someone asked you to explain the importance of spirituality, what would you say? How would you put it across in the hope of giving them a clear and helpful picture?

Religion

Introduction to Part II

Voltaire famously said that if God did not exist, it would be necessary to invent him. Part of what he meant by this is that religion meets, or at least seeks to address, a range of needs – personal, societal and political. Religion, then, is not simply a system of beliefs (or set of systems), it is a highly significant social phenomenon that has major implications at a number of levels.

It is therefore necessary to locate religion within a social and historical context, with certain key factors that shaped its development and how these put in motion such powerful influences that have shaped the political, social, psychological (and, of course, spiritual) landscape across the world.

This chapter explores the nature and significance of religion and reflects some of the complexities involved when it comes to pinning down a definition that applies to the full range of recognized religions.

We need to recognize the various roles played by religion in society over time, giving a clear picture of religion as a major social force as well as a pervasive influence on individual, family and community life, shaping expectations, prescribing moral frameworks, exercising power at a variety of levels and contributing – positively or negatively – to social justice.

Our aim is not to provide a detailed history, but, rather, to present a conceptual analysis that paints a picture of the part religion plays in shaping social life and personal experiences. In this way we will seek to cast light on the significance of religion for professional practice across the people professions.

DOI: 10.4324/9781003682318-17

As we made clear earlier, in discussing religion, we are neither promoting it nor disparaging it. What we are actually trying to do is to show that, whatever your own views about religion may be, ethically sound practice requires us to pay respectful attention to people's religious beliefs, practices and connections and how these shape their spirituality (how they express their chosen worldview), their life experience, the problems they encounter, the potential solutions and the potential for growth and development.

CHAPTER 15

Making sense of religion

Introduction

We noted earlier that spirituality is a 'slippery', hard-to-define concept. The concept of religion can similarly be so varied in interpretation that it is difficult to achieve an agreed common ground. This is not to deny the usefulness of various academic disciplines in helping us to understand the phenomenon of religion. The sociology of religion, for example, has made a powerful contribution to our understanding of these topics. Studies in lifespan development have also helped us to understand the complex web of our deep-seated human 'drives' and needs, as well as understanding some of the psychological aspects of religious experience. Any major reputable textbook from either of these disciplines will introduce the main themes and developments in this area. It is not within the purpose of this manual, however, to offer a detailed discussion of the main features of this complex academic terrain, although a brief synopsis will help to set the scene.

One aspect of the underlying theory base, however, is fundamental, namely a discussion of the main themes of religion in a way that has a direct bearing and relevance for the various disciplines across the people professions. This will inevitably include a focus on the issues of definition, and what are the 'touching places' that we can identify from our own practice.

So, before we go any further, it is important to attempt to develop a fuller understanding to build on the definition of religion offered by Canda et al. (2020), as mentioned at the end of the previous chapter. This involves issues that have fascinated sociologists and theologians alike, and it will come as no surprise to anyone new to this territory that the further we get into this issue of definitions, the more complex the debate becomes. Inevitably perhaps, some of the ideas we present will be hotly contested by sociological and theological specialists, but

DOI: 10.4324/9781003682318-18

without some understanding of the terms being used, there is a danger that they can mean different things to different people, with confusing results in practice.

This is a debate familiar to several professional groups. For example, Tanyi (2002), noting that spiritual care has been part of nursing history since ancient times, comments that:

> In the last few decades there has been a resurgence of spiritual discourse, as scientific-based approaches are not fully able to address many fundamental human problems such as persistent pain. Furthermore, people are searching for peace, meaningful lives.
>
> (p. 501)

At one level, of course, the question of definition, at least as far as religion is concerned, seems to be easily answered. By 'religion' is meant those major groupings within global societies that have particular names and identifiable sets of beliefs – for example, Islam, Christianity, Judaism, Buddhism and many more. Religion involves a systematic pattern of values, beliefs, symbols, behaviours and experiences that are shared by adherents and transmitted from one generation to the next through traditions (Canda et al., 2020).

Within such religious systems, there is generally a belief in the supernatural – a divine being or beings or spiritual forces that to some extent influence the behaviour of human beings. According to Robertson (1970, p. 47) religion: 'refers to the existence of supernatural beings that have a governing effect on life', although that would not apply to Buddhism.

It is important to recognize that the word 'religion' is often applied with equal ease to a much wider range of activities than the so-called mainstream religions. These include many New Religious Movements (NRMs). Hunt (2002) notes that there are now nearly 2,600 new religions, and comments that:

> contemporary NRMs... range from those such as the Unification Church, the Children of God, the Divine Light Mission, Krishna Consciousness, Scientology, Rastafarianism, Transcendental Meditation and the Rajneeshes. Many of these appear to have little in common.
>
> (pp. 146–7)

If, however, we add the observation that cult followings of sporting and contemporary music stars, not to mention the avid support of many football and other sporting teams, are also often described as being 'religions', then we see very acutely how important the problem of definition has become.

We begin to understand even more how utter bewilderment can set in for people who try to understand these issues and to explore what each of these various religious groups believes, but then give up the quest as 'mission impossible' – or just as likely, 'mission irrelevant'.

> **Key point**
>
> What is needed, in our view, is not a precise definition but a shared understanding of the key issues and their significance.

A way forward?

One way through this increasingly complex maze is to approach the issue from another direction, so that instead of asking ourselves what this or that particular religion stands for, or what its main tenets of faith are, we ask ourselves what a religion achieves for those who subscribe to it. This follows a tradition the sociologist Emile Durkheim developed, in which he argued that one of the main functions of religion is to promote the wellbeing, stability, and integration and social cohesion of society – in other words, focus attention on: What contribution does religion make to society? What function does it fulfil for those who subscribe to it, and for the society in which it is set?

A functionalist perspective on religion clearly has limitations. It does not do justice, for example, to the sense of awe and mystery and 'otherness' – theologians use the word 'transcendence' to point to this – which is at the heart certainly of the major monotheistic religions. Nor does it particularly help in the quest for testing the truth claims of particular religious groupings, or in grappling with the scepticism that grew out of the Enlightenment and which predicted the demise of religion in the advance of scientific rationalism. All of these issues are of great interest to sociologists of religion and theologians but lie outside the scope of this manual. Another criticism, however, which will be central to our discussion, is that it does not do justice to the ways in which, within some religions at least, there is a strong prophetic and critical challenge to the social order of the day. This is a theme we shall return to strongly.

People professionals, however, are likely to find the questions and issues that arise out of a functionalist perspective particularly useful, whether or not they themselves belong to a faith-based organization (FBO). It means that they can leave to one side, for the most part, the details of belief and doctrine a particular religious group happens to subscribe to, and ask instead questions such as:

- What does it mean for this person to belong to this FBO?
- What needs does it fulfil?
- What sense of meaning and purpose does it give to those who belong to it?
- What is the worldview they now subscribe to?
- What actions and activities flow from belonging to this group?

These are all crucial questions and illustrate what Patel et al. (1998) meant when they observed that, if you 'touch religion, you touch a person's deepest being' (p. ii). This is not to say that this will be true for everyone who has a religious dimension in their lives. Far from it – for some people, religious observances are no more than social rituals or conventions. What Patel et al. are referring to is when people take their religion with the utmost seriousness and allow it to shape their understanding of the world and their place within it. This is what Mannheim (1936) meant when he said:

> We belong to a group not because we are born into it, not merely because we profess to belong to it, nor finally because we give it our loyalty and allegiance, *but primarily because we see the world and certain things in the world the way it does.*
>
> (pp. 21–22, emphasis added)

And it is here, perhaps, that we find one of the major 'touching places' for much of the work that people professionals undertake. Whether it be in a counselling relationship where deep-seated issues of meaning and relationships are being explored; or in social work with its engagement with people in stressful, challenging, and at times abusive relationships; or in criminal justice work where people's behaviour raises deep issues of what drives them and gives them a 'buzz'; or in advice work where often people are overwhelmed by despair as a result of the escalating burden of debt and of trying to cope when the odds are stacked against them; or in youth work where young people are often trying to deal with the powerful tensions between their surging potential and limited opportunities; or in nursing where issues of health and illness, wellbeing and recovery, sickness and death are part of the daily round; or in an organizational context where employees are struggling with stress: in all these areas of work, the questions that have been suggested from a functionalist perspective on religion all have relevance.

Or do they? There is an immediate caveat here. If it is being suggested in all the areas of work outlined above that people who use these services all come from a religious background, then this would clearly need to be challenged, certainly in the UK context. The chances are that the majority of them would deny having any religious background or allegiance at all. But the questions still have relevance, which is why for many people the context for this whole debate needs to be widened considerably by bringing the concept of spirituality into the discussion.

Here we begin to see why we struggled to make a start with this discussion, and suggested that 'if I were you, I wouldn't start from here'. If religious concepts and 'holy talk' are increasingly being seen as the territory of the 'holy few', then spirituality, perhaps, fares no better in a secular society. As we have noted, spirituality is admittedly difficult to define, but Swinton (2001) argues that:

> whilst people may be becoming less religious, it would be a mistake to assume from that that they are necessarily becom less spiritual, or that

they are no longer searching for a sense of transcendence and spiritual fulfillment... spiritual beliefs and desires that were once located primarily within institutionalised religions have migrated across to other forms of spirituality... spirituality has broadened in meaning into a more diffuse human need that can be met quite apart from institutionalised religious structures.

(pp. 11–12)

As we saw in Part I, a lot of work has been done in this field already, not least in the United States of America, where for the past few decades academics and practitioners alike have been wrestling with these issues. Canda et al. (2020), for example, argue that, far from being an optional 'add-on', spirituality fulfils a unifying holistic function for every human being, whether or not they subscribe to a religious framework of belief. This led them to offer the definition we highlighted at the end of Chapter 14.

The big question for present purposes is whether these wider contexts of religion and spirituality need to be included in our professional practice, or whether we, and those who come to us, can get by perfectly well without them. Therefore, it may be helpful to lay alongside all of this two other comments that may help us engage with these issues, and to understand more clearly what Canda et al. are seeking to articulate.

Lloyd [Holloway] (1996) noted, in her work with parents who were struggling to cope with the death of a child, the frequency with which professional bodies encounter the 'Why?' question. This is the question that:

at times of great crisis and loss is thrown directly or indirectly at many people who work in human services, be they doctors, social workers, nurses, care assistants, counsellors, youth workers, leaders of faith communities... the big question – the really big question – is far less easy to handle.

(Moss, 2002, p. 35)

This 'big question' is the one that, at times, desperately seeks to find meaning in, and for, events that happen to us. This led Morgan (1993) to suggest that the search for meaning is ultimately what spirituality is all about, and to argue that: 'Human spirituality is to seek an answer to the question: "how can you make sense out of a world that does not seem to be intrinsically reasonable?"' (p. 6). Or to put it another way, spirituality asks us what our worldview is, and how we try to make sense of the things that happen to us.

As we discussed in Chapter 14, one common but misguided assumption is that spirituality has to be an individualistic, egocentric matter. Spirituality can also connect us with others and with the wider world more broadly, as our earlier discussion of connectedness has illustrated.

Two points deserve to be reaffirmed here. First, these are issues that affect everyone, whether or not they are articulated. Spirituality, in other words, is a sort of 'shorthand' way of asking the fundamental questions about ourselves: What makes us 'tick'? What is important to us? What gives us a sense of meaning and purpose in our lives? In short, it asks of people what their worldview is. These are issues that, in a wide variety of ways, people professionals grapple with in their everyday work, even if the concept of spirituality is rarely specifically mentioned. This 'wider context', as we have already highlighted, is far from being irrelevant to much of the work we undertake.

Second, spirituality has an outward-looking dimension to it. Here a litmus test of genuine spirituality is offered in the extent to which it 'fosters a sense of responsibility for... others'. At this point, there is considerable overlap between religious and spiritual perspectives, as evidenced by the testimony of people who have chosen, or felt inwardly compelled into, a social caring career, and for whom the claim by Canda et al. (2020) that 'spirituality is the heart of helping' rings true. Not that people professionals should claim a monopoly of this, however – far from it. This is an energy that is part of the potential of every human being. It is just that people professionals, whose work focuses on helping people tackle their problems and fulfil their potential, have the privilege of being instrumental in helping other people both to claim and to release that energy in their own lives, whether that is through counselling; advice work; engaging with young people; healing and nursing; management and leadership; or the many facets of social work practice.

This recognition of energy and potential to care for others has received a new emphasis in recent years, as many organizations have begun to recognize the contribution faith-based organizations can make, and are already making, to the enrichment of their local communities. Some significant work has been taking place to explore and develop the notion of social capital and how faith-based organizations can make serious contributions to this field (Kaasa, 2013). These developments locate spirituality within a framework of social justice and reintroduce the point made earlier about the prophetic strand in some religious traditions that challenges the ways in which society is structured, and which demands a more just and equitable social order.

This takes us into a broader definition of spirituality that can include religious perspectives within it, and certainly encompasses the search for meaning and purpose, but then goes on to ask the functionalist questions: What difference does all of this make to you and to what you do with your life? What impact does it have on how you treat other people, both individually and within communities and/or workplaces?

It is at this point that we can usefully return to our earlier definition of spirituality that should prove useful for professionals who wish to explore some of these central issues: *what we do to give expression to our chosen worldview.*

This worldview may be specifically religious – we may belong to a Christian, Jewish, Muslim, Hindu or one of many other faith-based communities, which give us a sense of community and purpose, and an outlook upon the world that shapes our thinking and our social action. It also encourages us to undertake certain activities, such as shared worship and prayer.

This worldview may most definitely not be religious – we may feel more comfortable with being agnostic or atheist or humanist. We may define our position as being existentialist – this too will shape our outlook upon the world and our social action, and what we choose to do and not to do to express our convictions (Thompson, 2007).

This worldview may be shared by others in very specific ways, in that we choose to belong to a group that shares, explores and develops the implications for social action; or we may hold it in isolation in a more individualistic way. In the end, the issues will be similar for us and for those we seek to work with.

What we cannot do is to ignore these issues or pretend that they are peripheral to our practice. Whether the practice and behaviours that spring from people's particular worldviews are liberating or oppressive is, of course, an issue of fundamental importance for practice.

Having reached this point in the discussion, one crucial insight should have been achieved. What we have been discussing is not a topic people professionals can somehow detach themselves from. The definition of spirituality being offered does not allow such tidy, sanitized boundaries to be drawn. Instead, it draws us all in, and encourages us to peer behind the labels we place upon each other and acknowledge that this is an enterprise in which we are all involved by virtue of being human. We all struggle to make sense of what happens to us and who is to say that one person's struggle is of greater or lesser value than another's? We owe each other the dignity and respect of recognizing that we are all on a similar journey of discovery.

This has a clear resonance with the tenets of best practice across various caring professions. The core values of dignity and respect; of recognizing that intrinsic value and worth of each individual (whether or not we subscribe to a religious perspective that holds that ultimate value is derived from a superior Being); of recognizing that loving, sacrificial caring for others is a potential within all people – these form the value base of how people professionals aspire to regard those who come to them for help, and how they themselves would wish to be regarded in return.

It also is a challenge to everyone working across the people professions to take a measure of responsibility for their own well-being in this regard. Practitioners are involved with people often at crisis points in their lives, where the big questions of meaning and purpose are raised, explicitly or implicitly. If they themselves as workers are not comfortable in this area, then they are not likely to feel able to be open and helpful to the people who need to feel listened to and valued at the very point where they need it most. But, it is precisely at this point that some workers are tempted to take flight:

> And each of them may well struggle with the 'Why?' question when it is asked, and each of them may feel it is best left to someone else to tackle – 'someone who knows about these things'. The assumption is that spirituality, however it is defined, is outwith the professional expertise

or even concern of most human services practitioners. As Lloyd [Holloway] (1997) so aptly observes, '... a spiritual dimension is not generally seen as part of the liberal-thinking, politically-aware social worker's anti-discriminatory tool kit' (p. 183)

(Moss, 2002, p. 36)

Our approach seeks to turn this observation on its head and argue that any people professional who fails to take the spiritual dimension of people's lives into account, or who fails to take it into account for their own lives, is not meeting the demands of best practice, and is not likely to be able to offer anything like the holistic service people are entitled to.

> **TIP!** Make sure that you find ways of ensuring that spirituality and religion are *integrated into* your work and not just an afterthought or something you consider occasionally.

A further implication of this understanding of spirituality needs to be considered. It might be thought from the argument developed so far that it is a case of 'anything goes', and that there are no moral or professional benchmarks to guide human behaviour or professional intervention, 'If my spirituality says it is OK to treat others in a particular way, who are you to deny me that right?'.

In some ways, this goes to the heart of some of the dilemmas that arise from practice situations, but it also raises the issue that has been touched on already, namely the extent to which religion and spirituality are life-enhancing or life-diminishing activities. It also raises the issue that is perhaps starkest in the three main monotheistic religions – Judaism, Christianity and Islam – about the extent to which the gendered and heterosexist nature of religious language and authority has been responsible for the systematic devaluing of women, and the refusal to acknowledge any validity for same-sex relationships.

Some of these issues are of such importance that it is necessary to consider them in the context of the theory base being explored here. Of necessity, the focus for this part of the discussion needs to be narrowed down to the three main monotheistic religions, for the following reasons. First, to attempt to cover every aspect of religion would prove too time and space consuming for the scope of this manual. Second, the issues can be most clearly identified and discussed by limiting the focus in this way. And third, for many people these issues are most appropriately laid at the door of these three religious systems. Finally, any principles established from this discussion can then be considered to see if they can be applied to any other religion.

Interestingly, the issues that need to be raised can all be understood from a similar functionalist perspective as has already been outlined above. The 'case against' these religions, if we may state it in this way, often has less to do with the truth claims each makes, or the details of the doctrinal dogmas each espouses, and far more to do with how the adherents of these religions have behaved towards others. It is precisely the apparent function of these religions to cause some of their followers to act in oppressive ways towards others that has led not only to suspicion, but to a 'root and branch' rejection of them by many people. It is perfectly possible, therefore, to understand how someone who has adopted this stance on moral or ethical grounds would find it difficult to agree with the definition of best practice outlined above, where a sensitivity to spirituality is being recommended.

It is at this point, however, that the worldview perspective comes into play again. Supporters of religion and their critics both have to find a way of coming to terms with the positive and negative aspects of religion, without simplistically and uncritically accepting or rejecting the 'whole package'. Looking at this theologically, there needs to be an understanding of good and evil within their worldview, where full justice is done to both. As Patel et al. (1998) so aptly put it:

> Human beings are able to commit unbelievable atrocities in the name of religion, and to rise to heights of courage and sacrifice for their faith. Any profession that aims to understand the underlying motivation of people should not ignore the place of religion in their lives.
>
> (p. 9)

Again, it is not our intention to rehearse all the arguments for and against the existence of a divine Being, or to explore the complex doctrinal subtleties within these three religions about the nature of good and evil. It will be helpful, however, as part of the theoretical underpinning, to examine at least some of the main issues that impinge upon practice.

Exercise 15

In what ways are a person's religious beliefs likely to affect their worldview and how they relate to other people? How might this lead to inter-faith conflicts?

CHAPTER 16

The major religions and their critics

Introduction

Here, we offer an overview of what has come to be known as the 'new atheism' and its critiques of the main religions and their tenets. In doing so, we seek to clarify the differences across religious, non-religious and anti-religious positions.

We examine and evaluate the critiques put forward by what philosopher Raymond Tallis (2018) calls the 'scorched-earth atheists' (Dawkins et al.) who self-identify as *anti*-religious. These views are compared with a non-religious approach that favours atheism, but without seeking to deny religious people the right to practise their faith.

The new atheists

This term is used to refer to a small group of writers who share a strongly anti-religious perspective and who rose to prominence in the first decade of the 21st century. They not only prefer to reject any religious beliefs for themselves, but actively campaign against religion, presenting it as an obstacle to social progress and a dangerous and destructive rejection of human reason.

This school of thought is most closely associated with the work of evolutionary biologist Richard Dawkins. His book, *The God Delusion*, first published in 2006, became a bestseller. In it he argued that the theory of evolution shows the fallacy of some basic religious beliefs (for example, that the world is only 10,000 years old). However, he goes on to argue that, as rational human beings, we should be rejecting the irrational ideas that religions tend to be based on.

The previous year Sam Harris had published a book called *The End of Faith: Religion, Terror, and the Future of Reason*. In it he argues that religious beliefs 'are leading us, inexorably, to kill one another' (p. 12). As a neuroscientist, he

 DOI: 10.4324/9781003682318-19

was proposing a more rational, scientific approach to life. In 2007 Christopher Hitchens, a highly respected journalist, published a book by the name of *God is Not Great*. The subtitle confirms the core message of the book: *How Religion Poisons Everything*. As we shall explore in Chapter 19 below, there are certainly problems that religion can be seen to contribute to in major ways, but perhaps the idea that it poisons everything is overstating the case.

Although generally referred to as atheists, these writers are more accurately seen as anti-theists. It is perfectly possible, and indeed quite common, to be an atheist (that is, someone who does not believe in God), while respecting other people's right to have religious beliefs if they so choose. Anti-theism, by contrast, is a polemical position that seeks to deny the validity of religion and therefore does not recognize people's right to have faith. While this may possibly be a legitimate philosophical position to hold at a theoretical level, it is highly problematic at the level of professional practice due to the values implications. That is, failing to recognize the significance of a person's religion (and thus in many ways their spirituality) can be seen as inadequate when it comes to treating people with respect and dignity and recognizing their right to self-determination. In some ways, it could even prove discriminatory and thus oppressive.

Key point

People professionals have the right to believe or not believe, as they see fit. But, an ethical line is crossed if an individual worker's lack of faith is used to deny others their right to believe or is in any other way disrespectful to their beliefs or associated practices.

Responding to the critique

Of course, such strongly worded views have not gone without countercriticism. Kathleen Jones writes at length about what she sees as the flaws in Dawkins' approach. Her view is summed up by her comment that: 'Richard Dawkins says that he hates dogma, and he says so in the most dogmatic terms' (2007, p. x). She is one of many people who have argued against the idea that scientific rationality somehow invalidates religious faith. There has been no shortage of people who have argued over time that the tendency to set science and religion against one another is a false dichotomy (Harrison, 2010; McGrath, 2015). It is perfectly possible, it has been argued time and again, to apply logic and rationality to those aspects of life that operate in this way, while relying on more intuitive experiential understanding of those aspects of life that do not fit neatly into scientific structures (or strictures). As Jones argues:

> If the evidence for a religious view is not scientific in the sense of being observable and provable, he [Dawkins] will have nothing to do with

it – though there is a great deal in the scientific field, from the Big Bang to dark energy, which he is well aware is neither observable nor provable. Science is allowed its mysteries, religion is not.

(p. 42)

It could be argued that dismissing religion on rational grounds is a largely pointless exercise, in so far as even atheists can recognize that religion does not necessarily claim to be rational. Or, in technical terms, religion can be understood as *metarational,* rather than irrational – that is, it is something that goes beyond rationality, not just simply lacks it. Indeed, this is parallel to the argument that science cannot displace philosophy, as there are many aspects of life that do not fit within a scientific paradigm (Tallis, 2018) – questions that cannot be answered empirically through observation and experimentation.

Foster (2009) is even stronger in rejecting Dawkins and his approach:

Richard Dawkins, seen by the TV-watching and paper-back reading public as representing mainstream science, is on the extreme jack-booted right wing of evolutionary biology. Very few in the trade think that things are as simple as he thinks they are. Real biology bristles with fascinating caveats.

(p. xiii)

Armstrong (2010) is also very critical of the tendency of the anti-theists to oversimplify religion and see it as a single monolithic entity, rather than the highly complex and diverse nature of what religion really is (as we shall discuss in Chapter 17 below).

So, what we have, then, is a school of thought that rejects religion wholesale, seeing it as a major factor in much of what is wrong in modern societies, while many people of faith have strongly challenged the basis of such claims, particularly in relation to the core idea that science negates the validity of religion. But, whatever our own views on the validity or otherwise of religious claims, we need to recognize just how important religion is to so many people and be appreciative of how much harm we could do if we were to try to impose our own view on others.

Exercise 16

What harm could be done if a professional were to disregard a person's religion simply because they do not have any religious beliefs of their own? Try to think of concrete examples of where this might occur and what the possible detrimental consequences could be.

CHAPTER 17

Religious diversity

Introduction

This chapter explores issues arising from the multiplicity of faith groups, approaches to religion and variations in religious experience. First of all, the focus is on diversity *across* religions in terms of the variety of minor religions (there are vast numbers of non-mainstream religions). This leads into a discussion of diversity *within* religions and warns against the danger of stereotypical understandings. Finally, there is a discussion of how spirituality (as a human phenomenon and not one that is specifically religious) acts as a linking thread across diverse religions.

Diversity across religions

Discussion of religion understandably tends to focus on the main religions that have massive numbers of followers, powerful institutions and a huge literature base. However, we should not allow this to fail to recognize that these are just the tip of the iceberg in terms of religions.

There is a parallel here with language. In the singular, the term 'language' is used in a very broad sense to refer to how we use speech and writing to communicate. In the plural, it refers to the wide range of different languages. Attention is largely focused on the most widely used languages, such as English, Spanish and Chinese, but there are actually between 6,000 and 7,000 languages across the world. According to the World Population Review, there is no definitive way of knowing how many religions there are in the world, but some estimates rate the number as over 4,000 (https://worldpopulationreview.com/country-rankings/religion-by-country).

DOI: 10.4324/9781003682318-20

Of course, from a practice point of view, no one is expected to be an expert in all of these religions or indeed any of them. However, what will often be important is to have at least a basic understanding of any key features of a person's or family's religion that may have a bearing on whatever situation you are dealing with.

TIP! Whenever you are involved in a situation where religious factors are significant, don't be afraid to be humble by explaining that you are not familiar with the religion concerned but you are willing to learn. People will generally be happy to tell you about their religion.

Diversity within religions

It is important to be aware that there is not only diversity across religions, but also considerable diversity within each religion. This can be seen to apply in three main ways. As we mentioned earlier, the new atheists have been criticized for presenting religion as a monolithic entity and thus failing to recognize key differences. For example, they dismiss religion on the basis of a lack of evidence of a supernatural being, but Buddhism is a religion that makes no such claims of the existence of a supernatural being.

First, there are sects or subgroupings within the same religion. A widely known example would be the divide between Catholicism and Protestantism in Christianity, with another layer of structure in terms of further divisions, such as Methodism, Lutheranism, Calvinism, and so on.

But even this is not the whole story as there are varieties of Orthodox Christianity, as well as a distinction between evangelical and non-evangelical Christians. And, of course, such diversity is not limited to Christianity – consider the differences between Sunni and Shia Muslims or between Orthodox and non-Orthodox Jews.

> **Key point**
>
> Given the diversity within religions, we need to be careful not to make assumptions about the lives and experiences of members of a particular faith community. This can be very misleading and potentially discriminatory.

Second, there will be different schools of thought. Theology is a complex and wide-ranging discipline, and while there are many examples of consensus, there is no shortage of competing perspectives on how, for example, a set of scriptures should be interpreted and acted upon. As with any other discipline, it would be naïve to expect no disagreements or differences of approach.

As part of this, there will also be differences between those who take religious teachings literally and those who subscribe to a particular religion but understand the sacred texts in metaphorical or narrative ways. For example, many Christians regard large elements of the Bible as symbolic and thus important, but not necessarily true in a literal sense.

Third, there will be differences in how individuals or families practise their religion. Catholics are expected to not use contraceptives, but this does not mean that all will abide by this. Similarly, many devout people, whatever their religion, will attend church, mosque or synagogue regularly, while other equally devout believers may rarely attend, if at all. The point we are making, therefore, is that people's lived experience of their religion will vary considerably. It is certainly not a case of 'one size fits all'. Again, we need to make sure that we are not relying on stereotypical assumptions.

Spirituality as a common theme

Religions generally involve institutionalized elements (liturgy, rituals, festivals, codes of ethics and so on) that differ from faith to faith and may change over time. However, what is common across religions is spirituality. As we noted earlier, a key feature of spirituality is the quest for meaning, the search for purpose and direction, a sense of connectedness and so on. Religions provide predefined frameworks of meaning that provide a basis for purpose and direction, and all within a context of connectedness, of being part of something bigger than yourself.

There is no doubt, then, that religion is highly significant when it comes to spirituality. It would be a significant mistake not to recognize this. However, it would be equally mistaken to assume that religion is the only way of expressing spirituality, meeting spiritual needs or rising to spiritual challenges.

As we have already emphasized, spirituality is much broader than religion. Consequently, when working with people of faith, we must not lose sight of how: (i) their religion is shaping their spirituality; and (ii) other non-religious elements may also be contributing. Similarly, when working with people of no faith, we must not assume that the absence of religion equates with an absence of spirituality. We need to use our critical thinking skills to engage with the complexities.

Exercise 17

If you were called upon to work with someone from a religious background that you are unfamiliar with, what questions would you want to ask them to find out what you need to know without being intrusive or disrespectful?

CHAPTER 18

The benefits of religion

Introduction

Religion is, of course, a source of considerable good in the world. Anti-religious approaches tend to focus on what are perceived as the problems associated with religion. This can produce an unbalanced view of what religions offer their adherents, in so far as it neglects consideration of the positive features of religion, such as social support, compassion, a strong sense of identity and so on.

This chapter provides an overview of these positive contributions. The main point of the chapter is to argue that there is a danger in attacking and undermining religion without giving full consideration to the benefits that would be lost in the event of the demise of religion. Chapter 19 will counterbalance the comments made here by looking at the problems associated with religion and how it has been practised historically and continues to be in the present day.

As we have already emphasized, we are not trying to promote religion or attack it. Our aim is an educational one of helping people professionals recognize the importance of religion and spirituality and appreciate the dangers of neglecting the issues that arise in this regard.

The positive contribution of religion: ten key points

What follows is by no means an exhaustive list, but should be sufficient to make the point that, despite its critics, religion does make a positive contribution to society.

1. There can be no denying that interest in religion generally, and membership of faith communities in particular, is still strong worldwide (Micklethwait and Wooldridge, 2009). At the very least this indicates that we are not

DOI: 10.4324/9781003682318-21

dealing with a marginalized activity, but that religion still is a major force within the world. It matters to very many people.

2. Many religious communities are harnessing a lot of energy and commitment, serving not just their local communities in the fight against poverty and social exclusion but also on a larger worldwide canvas with anti-poverty work and political lobbying on behalf of political prisoners.

3. Faith communities undertake a significant amount of pastoral and caring work within their local communities, including work with young people, families, unemployed people and older people. They continue to offer pastoral care to people at the end of their lives and through times of bereavement and sickness.

4. Some sections of the multicultural communities in the UK not only positively identify with their faith communities but also see them as an important network and resource against the racism of the wider community. The anti-racist role of faith communities in consolidating and celebrating cultural identities is significant.

5. Many faith communities are in the vanguard of multicultural developments within local communities to help build greater tolerance and mutual respect between groups. Some strongly encourage their members to play an active part in local politics for the benefit of their communities.

6. Many multi-faith communities play a lead role in developing a wide range of cultural activities in their local areas. They play a part in developing 'social capital' – that is, the social resources that people can benefit from.

Key point

Developing social capital is an important part of effective practice in the people professions. Whatever difficulties and challenges people may face in their lives, the more social support they have, the more successful they are likely to be in addressing the issues they face.

---

7. There are examples of faith-based organizations undertaking specific projects to improve the quality of life for the whole community they are part of. They play a role in developing social capital and in raising and tackling social justice concerns within their local communities.

8. FBOs still have a role to play within education at local and national levels and are consulted by government on a range of issues of national and international concern. They also from time to time challenge government policy and seek to provide moral leadership and guidance.

9. There is research that suggests some positive correlations between religious faith/belonging to a faith community and psychological wellbeing and can also have benefits in terms of health (Mochon et al., 2011).

10. Religion provides a counterbalance to a narrowly materialistic approach to life and offers more spiritually fulfilling understandings of human experience that can enrich people's lives. Bauman (2005) explores issues of consumerism and argues that a modern sense of self-identity is inextricably linked with what we buy and the range of products that we choose to surround us. In this sense 'we are what we buy', and the bewildering range of choices allows us to express our individuality, and 'to play the game'. Not that everyone can 'play the game' of course – that requires resources that are not available to everyone. Bauman argues that religion, especially in its fundamentalist forms, is a threat to this consumerism upon which much of modern capitalism depends, because it provides 'a supposed remedy for a sense of individual incapacity provoked by the consumer society' (cited in Henery, 2003, p. 1108). With a deft tweak to George Bernard Shaw's infamous idea, we might now proclaim with tongue in cheek, following Bauman's analysis, that 'those who can, buy; those who can't, turn to religion'. As Henery notes:

> Religion is a threat to consumer capitalism because it takes people 'out of the game'. Its truths are static and unchanging and therefore incompatible with a continually revisable environment of knowledge. The conduct and lifestyle it promotes does not emphasise a lifestyle of product acquisition… Religion threatens modernity and consumer capitalism by allowing people to opt out of these demands, and – worse – provides a form of communal legitimation for such a choice.
>
> (p. 1108)

This kaleidoscope of activities illustrates the wealth of resources available in local communities through faith-based organizations, much of which goes unacknowledged and unsung. It is not to suggest, however, that these are the only care or support activities that happen in local communities, or that people who do not belong to faith communities do not also actively participate in such work – far from it. It is simply to make the point that FBOs do contribute positively, creatively and significantly to society at all levels, and deserve for that reason, if for no other, to be taken seriously by people professionals.

Finally, it is instructive to reflect on the ways in which religious and spiritual convictions have played a significant part in the development of many of the social care agencies that are now part of the fabric of our society – although admittedly 'for the social work profession in the West, the impact of Christianity on social work has become a barely remembered part of the professional heritage' (Bowpitt, 1998, p. 676).

Nevertheless, much of the early impetus towards social work came from religiously motivated philanthropy. The origins of the Probation Service, once committed to 'advise, assist and befriend', may be found in the 'Police Court Missionaries' who 'loitered creatively' at the magistrates' courts in order to help and guide those who had fallen foul of the criminal law. These became probation officers in 1907, 'although it was many years before the statutory probation service disentangled itself from its religious and voluntary roots' (Williams, 1995, p. 23). The strong religious convictions of many probation officers may be evidenced by the fact that prayers were only dropped from the annual general meeting of the National Association of Probation Officers after bitter arguments in the late 1970s (Williams, 1995, p. 41).

Some of the foundational principles of social work, counselling, and the active listening skills that have now permeated much professional practice, may be traced to the work of Biestek (1957), who was himself a Roman Catholic priest. Faith communities have pioneered work with young people, while the role of chaplains within hospitals has long been an accepted feature of medical life.

This brief snapshot illustrates the wealth of resources available to local communities through their FBOs, the potential for which has still to be fully realized.

Exercise 18

What religion-based resources are available to you in your geographical area and your area of work? It will be helpful for you to research this and make a list of possibilities for future reference. Our experience is that people are often unaware of the local possibilities.

CHAPTER 19

The problems of religion

Introduction

In Chapter 18, we saw that religion plays an important positive role in society in at least ten ways. However, it has to be recognized that religion also brings with it a number of problems, including very serious ones. Our focus in this chapter, therefore, is on the other side of the coin, the negatives that counterbalance the various positives.

The Dalai Lama (2011) makes the important point that: 'Though religion certainly has the potential to help people lead meaningful and happy lives, it too, when misused, can become a source of conflict and division' (p. xii). Similarly, Onfray (2011) states that:

> In the name of God, as centuries of history attest, the three monotheisms have caused unbelievable rivers of blood to flow! Wars, punitive operations, massacres, murders, colonialism, the elimination of entire cultures, genocides, crusades, inquisitions, and today's global terrorism.
>
> (p. 62)

In this chapter we therefore review some key examples and consider the characteristics of religion that can contribute to such problems – for example, religious exclusivism: the belief on the part of members of a particular religion that theirs is the only true religion. This can lead to not only disrespecting other religious groups but also destructive acts, including violence, towards other such groups.

Religion as a contributor to social problems

Echoing the structure of Chapter 18, we now present a brief overview of ten problems associated with religion (or at least with the way religions have been practised).

DOI: 10.4324/9781003682318-22

1. Sustaining inequality and oppression is a charge that has been levelled against religion on many occasions. 'Know your place, accept the status quo and you will be rewarded later' is a sentiment strongly associated with at least certain forms of belief, reflecting the view that the passivity encouraged is a form of social control, in so far as it allows the wheels of power to keep turning in favour of the dominant groups.

   Of course, there is the counterargument that 'liberation theology', as a contribution to developing social justice, has actually been instrumental in challenging oppressive regimes and changing the balance of power (Gutierrez, 2001).

2. The conflicts and wars associated with religion are perhaps the most salient example of a problem seen to arise from religion. Indeed, the impact of major warfare and disasters, especially in the 20th and early 21st centuries, has been a further major contributor to the distrust and rejection of religion. This has had several strands to it. The impact of two world wars upon some people's theological understanding or the world – their worldview – was profound. 'Where is God in all of this?' is an example of a big 'Why?' question that many people asked and found their faith and theology lacking. The impact of the Holocaust had repercussions not just for Jewish theology and post-Holocaust theologians, but for many more people whose religious understanding could not accommodate such atrocities. The level of violence in Israel/Palestine causes many people to ask similar questions. Equally daunting has been the development of fundamentalist regimes and contemporary 'crusades' in the name of Islam, for example. Despite strenuous attempts to dissociate the heart of Islam from these political excesses, and to seek to avoid Islamophobia wherever possible, the impact of these events cannot be underestimated. Groups of militants continue to do what they have done since time immemorial and have called upon the name of their 'God' to support them in their territorial imperialism.

   There are many other points throughout the world where the religions involved may be different, but the issue remains fundamentally the same: imperialism with a religious cloak. And it is the poor and the dispossessed, the refugee and the homeless who are the helpless victims.

3. The role of women in certain religious areas has also been a major cause of concern for many. There are several strands to this theme. First, in the various holy books that serve as the authoritative baseline for the three main Abrahamic religions – the Torah and the Talmud for Jews; the Bible for Christians; and the Qu'ran for Muslims – the role of women is frequently stated as being subservient to men. This has had profound repercussions for family life; for women's freedom to make decisions about their bodies and for political power and authority. With some notable exceptions, the world of religion is still male dominated, and the sexism that exists in society generally is seen to be even stronger within many faith communities.

Undoubtedly, there is now a serious attempt being made by feminist theologians to distinguish between the true heart of each of these religions, in which women enjoy equal status and dignity, and the gendered nature of the holy books and the traditions that have bolstered male dominance down the centuries. Some parts of the Christian church have now accepted women priests and ministers, but resistance to this is still very deep seated.

4. Human sexuality is another contentious area. One issue that continues to cause consternation is the way in which the major religions by and large continue to deny the validity of same-sex relationships and actively ostracize LGTBQ+ people from their congregations. Again, the holy books are used to justify this position, and it is an issue that is often characterized by a crusading vehemence. Nevertheless, there are many examples of gay Christian clergy continuing to exercise their leadership role, but the comfort zone for them is very slender, and many gay people involved in faith communities are still afraid to 'come out' for fear of reprisals and rejection.

It is clear that, on this issue and the role of women, the fundamental value of celebrating diversity is at odds with much traditional teaching on these issues within these faith communities.

5. One further nail in the coffin of religion, as far as many people are concerned, is the many examples of abuse or harmful behaviours within faith communities. The various cases of sexual abuse against children by religious leaders, some of which have been covered up for decades, cause scandal and outrage amongst the population at large. Some of the child abuse scandals have had religious overtones to them. The Victoria Climbié inquiry, for example, revealed that a pastoral leader had 'diagnosed' demon possession and had not notified the authorities of the abuse; and the account of social work supervision including prayer and bible study caused shock and dismay to the profession at large. Other harmful practices include female genital mutilation, forced marriages and religion-based honour killings.

6. Proselytizing is a further issue that has attracted criticism. There is a legitimate concern that workers who have a religious allegiance may use opportunities that arise in their work to seek to persuade vulnerable people to adopt their religious point of view. Although such conduct is highly likely to be forbidden in codes of conduct, this remains an area of concern for some that workers who belong to faith communities may not be sufficiently scrupulous in working within these guidelines.

7. Terrorism has been a major concern since the 9/11 attacks in the United States. The association between Islam as a religion of peace and Islam*ism* as a terrorist ideology has created a strong antipathy to religion for many people. The high level of media attention to terrorism has played a part in fuelling Islamophobia, further reinforcing the idea of religion as a source of evil. The terrorist activities of far-right groups who often embrace evangelical

beliefs of one sort or another are a further reason for so many people to mis-trust religion or even reject it altogether.

8. The tendency for religions to lay down set patterns of beliefs, thoughts, feel-ings and expected actions is, for many people, a reason to criticize religion and see it in negative terms. Blocking human potential by placing artifi-cial strictures on people's lives can be seen as a significant problem. In par-ticular, the predominance in much religious practice of generating fear and guilt has been a source of criticism from people in many quarters over an extended period of time.

9. In a similar vein, the prescriptive elements of religion are open to criticism for discouraging critical and creative thinking. Major breakthroughs in the arts, sciences and commerce can be seen to have arisen from critical and creative thinking – from questioning taken-for-granted assumptions and 'thinking outside the box'. Those aspects of religion that emphasize conformity and uniformity therefore come at quite a price in terms of lost opportunities for progress.

10. While we were earlier critical of the new atheists for their tendency to see scientific rationality as the be all and end all of human understanding, we must also recognize that some forms of religious belief reject science and rationality because they see these as denials of religion, rather than as poten-tially complementary ways of making sense of the world. For example, as McGrath (2015) argues, Christianity and evolutionary theory can be under-stood as compatible, and so rejecting the latter serves to hold back scientific progress and the benefits it can bring.

TIP! Be careful not to overgeneralize here. We are talking about certain aspects of certain religions at certain times. These are complex issues that need to be considered carefully

Overview

The problems associated with religion, as briefly outlined here are of significant proportions. The examples given illustrate that religion is a powerful social force that, in certain circumstances, can do immense harm – they are not the innocent pastimes that some people claim. They can indeed at times be extremely destruc-tive and an example (some would argue) of the old tag 'corruptio optimi pessima' (take something that is essentially good, and corrupt it or use it for ignoble ends, and the outcome is the worst possible that you can imagine).

Against this backcloth it is easy to see how issues of religion have at the very least been ignored on many training syllabuses and have been seen by many practitioners across a wide spectrum as being irrelevant, pathological or even dangerous. If we are to do justice in our practice to the complexities of religion in people's lives, then we need to be aware of and tuned in to both the positives and negatives of religion, as outlined in this chapter and the previous one.

One important point to be aware of is that there is nothing in any of these problems that is inherent in religion or an inevitable part of faith. We shall return to this point in the next chapter.

Exercise 19

How might the negatives associated with religion lead to religious discrimination? What steps could be taken to address any such concerns?

CHAPTER 20

Religion and morality

Introduction

To many people morality is synonymous with religion, based on the misguided view that only faith-based morality has any basis in reality. This is just one of the complexities associated with religion and morality. This chapter explores some of the other complexities and, in particular draws on the influential morality framework developed by social psychologist Jonathan Haidt (2013).

How morality relates to religion

The relationship between religion and morality is a complex that can be traced back to ancient times. Religious doctrines have long served as ethical frameworks for defining what is to be defined as right or wrong. Indeed, the connection between religious beliefs and moral expectations is very strong indeed – consider, for example, Christianity's ten commandments or Islam's five pillars.

However, increased secularization has contributed to a weakening of religion's influence in the field of morality. We have also seen a degree of modernization in terms of religion-based values – for example, a greater level of acceptance of same-sex relationships in some quarters. None the less, religious narratives, rituals and communities continue to reinforce specific moral values and, in doing so, provide a framework for ethical decision making, and so the influence of religion should not be underestimated. For example, many people who have rejected the religion of their family and/or community that they were exposed to in their upbringing may well continue to base their sense of morality on the moral values that they grew up with and have thus internalized. In this regard, some Jewish people reject Judaism but continue to live according to Jewish culture.

It is generally – but not exclusively – the case that religious texts are regarded as divine pronouncements, with religious leaders being seen as moral authorities,

DOI: 10.4324/9781003682318-23

human but guided by divine insights embodied in sacred texts and accepted interpretations of them. In terms of ontological security, as discussed earlier, this structure, stability and moral guidance can be helpful, a source of confidence and reassurance. However, rigid interpretations and intolerance towards dissenting views can give rise to significant problems. This can apply at a macro level (consider, for example, the problems with religious conflicts discussed earlier, such as sectarianism). There can also be problems at the micro level when people's creativity, intellectual development and thus life chances can be unnecessarily stifled by overly strict interpretations of religious doctrine – for example, Ali (2016) contends that there is nothing in the Koran that justifies or requires the restrictions on women commonly associated with Islam.

Religious morality needs to be recognized as a two-edged sword. While, on the one hand, it can make positive contributions to social harmony and civilized relations towards others, it can also be exclusionary, judgemental and even violent (consider the phenomenon of honour killings, for example). Other examples would include religious persecution and, as we noted earlier, religion-based wars and conflicts.

TIP! Be aware of your own moral values when considering other people's. Consider also the wider context of religious values. Without this reflection, it is very easy to become judgemental.

Haidt's moral framework

Haidt (2013) proposes a framework that is based on six themes expressed in pairings of positive and negative, with different moral-political traditions reflecting different emphases within this sixfold framework. The pairings are:

- Care vs. harm;
- Fairness vs. cheating;
- Loyalty vs. betrayal;
- Authority vs. subversion;
- Sanctity vs. degradation; and
- Liberty vs. oppression.

The Abrahamic religions of Judaism, Christianity and Islam emphasize loyalty to the divine and the religious community, often through rituals and communal practices. The pairing of sanctity vs. degradation is particularly significant within faith communities. For example, many religions have dietary and other taboos and rituals of purification that reflect a commitment to sacredness and the avoidance of defilement. For example, the Jewish concept of *kashrut* (kosher dietary laws) and the Islamic concept of *halal* are moral requirements based on perceptions of purity.

Interestingly, Haidt's framework suggests that political liberals tend to place particular emphasis on the care vs. harm and fairness vs. cheating pairings, while conservatives tend to value all six foundations more equally, including loyalty, authority and sanctity. This difference can go some way towards explaining some of the moral disagreements between religious and secular individuals. Religious conservatives, he argues, are more likely to prioritize loyalty to their faith community, respect for religious authority and adherence to traditional moral values, while secular liberals may prioritize individual autonomy, social justice and the valuing of diversity. While this does seem to make sense up to a point, we should bear in mind that these are complex multidimensional issues, and so we should be very careful not to oversimplify them.

Reflective moment

How would you see your own values in terms of this sixfold framework? Which might you prioritize and why?

Religious diversity

Buddhism, Hinduism and other eastern religions can be seen to have a different approach to the relationship between religion and morality. A key part of Buddhism, for example, is the promotion of compassion, mindfulness and the avoidance of harm. *Karma* refers to the idea that what we do today has consequences – good or ill – for our future lives in terms of reincarnation, promoting ethical behaviour. The Hindu concept of *dharma* places a duty to behave in certain ways and thus serves as a basis of morality.

Eastern religions tend to place great emphasis on inner transformation and spiritual development as foundation of ethical approaches to life and to each other.

Key point

As with any approach to morality, it should not be assumed that members of a faith community will necessarily abide by its moral code. We do not have to look far to find examples of people behaving in ways that are far from consistent with the teachings of their religion. Again, we need to avoid oversimplification.

Conclusion

In working with people of different faiths and none, we need to be aware that their actions and attitudes are likely, in part at least, to be influenced by the moral code into which they have been socialized as part of their upbringing. Having such knowledge and awareness will help us to be better equipped to understand, and relate to, the situation people find themselves in and what it means to them.

One aspect of religion and morality that we have not addressed is the role of liberation theology. This topic is a good example of how morality and politics intertwine, and so it is one that we shall focus on in the next chapter when we examine the relationship between religion and politics.

Exercise 20

What are the three most prominent religions where you work (or are likely to work)? How might each of these be relevant to your work in terms of the moral foundations underpinning them?

CHAPTER 21

Religion and politics

Introduction

Politics is often referred to as the art of the possible, and what is possible in any given set of circumstances will depend on the prevailing framework of values and beliefs, including religion, and so straight away we can see a connection between religion and politics. But politics is also generally understood to be about power and how it is exercised, and so again we can see that religion is part of this, in so far as religious bodies commonly have a significant role to play in how power is exercised, whether through formal mechanisms (bishops in the House of Lords in the UK, for example) or informally through the pervasiveness of religious beliefs within particular communities.

This chapter examines some important issues arising from the relationship between religion and politics but, as this is such a vast and complex topic, our review will be far from comprehensive and therefore necessarily selective.

The historic picture

The relationship between religion and politics is, of course, not new. We can trace the role of religion in politics back to ancient times, with many early societies being governed by religious bodies. Consider, for example, the role of Christianity in the Roman Empire after the initial objection to it subsided or the role of Islam in the Umayyad Caliphate that spread across the Middle East, North Africa and Spain between 661 and 750 CE.

As we noted earlier, religious divisions have been the source of wars and conflicts over centuries, and so this is a further example of how religion has been integral to the political sphere for a very long time. Some societies historically have even seen their leaders as divine – for example, Mesopotamia and Ancient

DOI: 10.4324/9781003682318-24

Egypt. In medieval Europe, the Catholic Church wielded significant political influence, with popes crowning emperors and dictating policy. Similarly, in many eastern traditions, rulers can be understood to have a mandate from heaven, as in Confucianism, for example.

Separation of church and state

The First Amendment of the Constitution of the United States of America enshrines the separation of church and state. So, while Christianity is the predominant religion there, the Constitution recognizes the right of all religions to exist. Many other countries, while not necessarily making the point as explicitly as the USA does, have a similar recognition that church and state need to be kept separate. Consequently, in such countries, while one or more religions may be powerful forces within society, the operation of the government and related state organizations remain secular.

Key point

It would be naïve not to recognize that religious beliefs, organizations and pressure groups have a powerful impact on political decision making, policy formulation and implementation.

There are, none the less, countries where no such church-state divide exists, where religious values play a central role. For example, Iran does not uphold the separation of church and state principle. It is an overtly Islamic republic where the Supreme Leader is a religious cleric who holds significant authority over both government and religious affairs. Islamic law (Sharia) plays a central role in legislation and the state enforces religious doctrine in governance.

The influence of religion on politics

The role of religion in shaping political thinking and events varies across time and space. At one extreme, there are theocracies where religious law has primacy and religious leaders hold significant political power. The Vatican City is a clear example of this and some Islamic states certainly have elements of this in terms of how they function on a day-to-day basis. This contrasts starkly with, for example, France which has its principle of *laïcité* – that is a strict enforcement of separation of religion from government affairs, ensuring that the state remains neutral and free from religious influence. As with the US constitution, it guarantees freedom of belief. The principle has its roots in the Enlightenment and the French Revolution as a result of the struggle against the political power of the Catholic Church.

Between these two extremes lie many variations, but what should be clear is that: (i) there will be differences in the relationship between church and state both historically and geographically; and (ii) even where religion is forbidden from influencing politics directly, there will be many subtle and not-so-subtle ways in which religious issues will play a part. An example of this would be the political significance of abortion in the United States, in part underpinned by the influence of evangelical Christianity on politics that has become increasingly prominent. The involvement of Evangelical Christians, with their strong views on abortion, same-sex marriage and other social issues, in the Republican Party has been especially notable, despite the separation of church and state principle (Smith, 1998). This highlights the complexity of the relationship between religion and politics.

Religion and politics can also be seen to mix in other religions. Buddhism, for example, has played a significant role in political movements in places like Myanmar and Sri Lanka, with a focus on promoting peace and social justice. Hinduism has its own political influence, with some supporters working to bring Hindu values into government and society. Judaism, with its long history of facing persecution and its strong focus on social justice, has also shaped political conversations, especially around topics like Israel and human rights.

TIP! In dealing with religious matters, don't forget to bear in mind that what counts is not only the faith concerned, but also how the people concerned actually practise it. There can be considerable variety in terms of how doctrines are interpreted and put into practice.

Liberation theology

Liberation theology is a Christian movement that emerged in the 1960s in Latin America. It sought to address social injustice and oppression through faith. Influenced by Marxist analysis, it critiqued capitalism while reinterpreting Christian doctrine to advocate for people living in poverty. Key figures like Gustavo Gutiérrez, Leonardo Boff and Archbishop Óscar Romero emphasized a number of key principles, including:

- *Preferential option for the poor* – A view that God has a special concern for marginalized and oppressed people. It places a duty on Christians to prioritize the needs of poor people in making social, economic and political decisions, as part of a commitment to social justice and equality.
- *Structural sin* – The concept of sin is generally understood in individualistic terms as personal moral failings. By contrast, structural sin refers to systemic injustices embedded in social, economic, and political structures. It fits well with modern conceptions of anti-discriminatory practice, with its recognition of the injustices associated with inequality, exploitation and oppression maintained by systemically and institutionally, rather than just by personal actions.

- *Active social engagement* – Liberation theology emphasizes that faith should lead to action. Instead of being passive, Christians are urged to engage in social and political struggles, working to dismantle oppressive structures and create a more just society.

While its influence has waned since the 1980s, in large part due to its association with marxist thought and its failed experiments in the former Soviet Union regime and elsewhere, liberation theology continues to inspire contemporary movements. Its focus on economic justice remains very relevant in contemporary discussions of neoliberalism and the significant inequalities it generates. It demonstrates the power of religious thought to influence politics and be a driving force in bringing about political and social change.

> **Reflective moment**
>
> Has religion affected your political views in any way? If so, how? If not, why do you think that is?

Religious discrimination

Of course, any form of discrimination involves power and therefore has a political element to it. Discrimination on the grounds of religion is no exception. We therefore need, as part of our consideration of the relationship between religion and politics, to consider – albeit briefly – the significance of religious discrimination.

Such discrimination can be seen to operate in four main ways:

- *Anti-religious discrimination* This refers to a general religious intolerance, a tendency to treat negatively anything connected with faith or faith communities.
- *Discrimination against a particular religion* The two most prominent examples of this are anti-semitism (Shabi, 2024) and Islamophobia (Warsi, 2024). These are again highly complex and sensitive issues characterized by major misunderstandings and misrepresentations that have given rise to considerable ill-feeling and hostility, especially in relation to anti-Zionism and the actions of the Israeli state being confused with anti-semitism (Neuberger, 2019).
- *Sectarianism* As discussed earlier, this relates to antagonism between two sections (or sects) of the same religion.
- *Anti-secular discrimination* This describes circumstances where members of a particular faith act negatively towards people who reject religion. In some countries, atheism is seen as a form of sin or even crime (https://humanists.uk/2022/12/08/over-70-of-people-live-in-countries-that-sev

erely-discriminate-against-the-non-religious-report/#:~:text=Over%20
70%25%20of%20the%20world's,situation%20has%20been%20getting%20
worse).

In some ways, religious discrimination overlaps with racism, but it can also
exist without any racial or ethnic considerations, and so it needs to be considered as part of the broader field of anti-discriminatory practice in a context of intersectionality – that is, the common interaction of different forms of
discrimination.

Conclusion

The relationship between religion and politics is a complex, multifaceted and
constantly evolving one. In terms of professional practice and management, we
do not need to develop any particular expertise in this area, but we do need to be
tuned in to the significance of these complexities, as they may well have a bearing on aspects of practice at times, especially when working with people whose
religious and/or cultural background may be different from our own and may be
playing a significant role in the circumstances we are dealing with.

It is to be hoped that this chapter has also reinforced our key message that,
regardless of our own religious or secular view, where religion matters to the
people we are working with, then it needs to matter to us in terms of we assess
the situation and how we respond to it. As Haidt (2013) puts it: 'Politics and religion are both expressions of our underlying moral psychology, and an understanding of that psychology can help to bring people together' (p. xii).

Exercise 21

A linking theme between religion and politics is power. Consider where and
how power issues arise when religion and politics come together in various
ways.

CHAPTER 22

Religion today and tomorrow

Introduction

Having reviewed some of the main pluses and minuses of religion and the relationship between morality and politics we now want to provide an overview of where we feel religion is up to today. We begin by considering some theoretical ideas that help us make sense of religion. We then look at the differences between how religion is understood theoretically and how it actually manifests itself in practice. Finally, we reaffirm the importance for the people professions of having at least a basic understanding of religion, regardless of our own views on faith.

Our aim in this chapter is to give you a foundation of understanding in order to give you a greater degree of confidence in dealing with the complex and sensitive issues that arise in relation to religion.

Laying theoretical foundations

Without doubt, the work of Weber occupies a central position in the understanding of the role of religion in society. He studied and wrote extensively about religion, including studies of ancient Judaism, Hinduism, and Buddhism, as well as Christianity. His famous study, *The Protestant Ethic and the Spirit of Capitalism*, published in 1904, adopted a different approach from earlier writers on religion like Feuerbach and Marx, in that he believed that religion could be seen as a positive and creative force for social change. Indeed, he argued that the values deriving from the Protestant Christian worldview provided a core motivation to the economic transformation of the West. In a nutshell, the drive to succeed materially was a desire to serve God, and material success was evidence of divine favour.

Weber also emphasized the potential revolutionary nature of Christianity in challenging and seeking to overthrow unjust social structures, although there is

DOI: 10.4324/9781003682318-25

always the associated risk that armed struggles conducted from religious motives can be particularly oppressive.

The role that religion – or at least religious organizations – might occupy within society has also been highlighted by some political theorists, albeit indirectly. The work of Etzioni (1995), for example, and the rise of the concept of communitarianism have had a significant impact on British society in recent decades. Here the emphasis has been not only to challenge the individualism encouraged by neoliberalism, but also to develop a society where social welfare is regarded as a positive strength, and where a variety of community groups, as well as individuals, have a key role to play. With governments increasingly feeling overloaded in their ability to pay for and deliver a range of public services, the role of religious organizations has been brought to the forefront of the debate. As in America, faith communities in Britain and in Europe are beginning to be seen as key players in the provision of services to the community.

Governments are finding it increasingly difficult to resource the welfare programmes demanded by their electorates. But, in turning to the private sector for funding initiatives, they are finding that the clash between public service and profit is creating a resistance to the generation of adequate resources. If the private sector won't pay and the government can't pay, it is the government who ends up the loser, as its credibility with the electorate to deliver its promises is undermined. In this potential vacuum, faith communities are being encouraged to develop an increasingly active role as the provider of welfare services within their communities. Issues of doctrinal truth mean little in this context: if a faith community can deliver the goods, they will get the contract.

These wider political contexts are important to the discussion, in so far as they set the scene for ways in which faith communities are becoming increasingly recognized as key players in community regeneration and development.

Another theorist who deserves some attention at this point is Ulrich Beck who is perhaps best known for his writings around a 'risk society'. For Beck, managing risk is the prime feature of global order, which is marked by new risks posed by the development of science and technology – the debate about the risks of genetically modified crops is an example of this.

This analysis of the 'risk society' can work in two ways, of course. For some, there is an added frisson of excitement and challenge as they move through uncharted waters. New forms of political pressure groups emerge to challenge the view that decisions about the future of society can safely be left in the hands of the politicians. Within the framework of spirituality we are suggesting in this manual – that spirituality is what we do to express our chosen worldview – there is clearly plenty of scope for people to develop new patterns of meaning and purpose. The bewildering rise of 'new age' religious movements may be understood against the background of this increasingly risk-filled society; indeed, it is possible to view risk as a positive and creative opportunity, and maybe for some a prophetic challenge to traditional political structures.

For others, by contrast, there is an increased sense of unease in a 'risk society' that can push them towards those faith communities that offer a deeper sense of security, meaning and purpose in life. For them, religion remains perhaps something more akin to the 'haven from the storm' that Marx critiqued so long ago. In an uncertain, risky world, many people actively seek and are hugely relieved to find organizations that offer a sense of security that they believe both outlasts and underpins an otherwise transient society. This would explain the rise of fundamentalism within both Christianity and Islam, and its increasing popularity.

Reflective moment

How did you learn about religion? How did it feature in your upbringing? What impact does it have on your life now?

At their best, religion and spirituality can both recognize and release power and potential within people to transcend experiences of great pain and loss. We often refer to the idea of 'rising above' the problems and traumas that can happen to us. In this sense, we can understand the positive and enabling aspects of religion and spirituality as both nurturing and releasing within people a greater resilience to cope with life in its darkest moments.

This is another example where it is possible to make creative links with a theoretical perspective that enables us to take seriously the positive contribution religion can make to people's lives.

Gaps between theory and practice

We noted in Chapter 19 that there are many problems associated with the practice of religion. The new atheists use this to justify their wholesale rejection of religion. However, the picture is quite complex, as the problems associated with religion are not necessarily inherent in religion. Grayling (2004) highlights how problems arise from poorly understood philosophies (including religions) and the way they are used:

> many if not indeed most of the conflicts and turmoils, revolutions and resurgences that mark the epochs of history are driven by philosophies – often half-baked and usually less than half understood, dreadfully oversimplified when turned into slogans for mass consumption, and invariably destined to harden into stone if adopted by ruling establishments, so that to disagree with them is to risk all forms of punishment up to and including death.
>
> (pp. 145–6)

This reflects a distinction made in linguistics between langue and parole. Both words can be translated from the French as 'language', but in different senses. Langue refers to language at the abstract level, including such elements as syntax, semantics, phonology and so on – the different components of how language works. Parole, by contrast, refers to how language is actually used in practice. Actual speech will commonly include mistakes, false starts, incomplete sentences and so on. For example, first-language speakers of English will generally be well aware that 'things' is plural and should therefore take a plural verb, as in 'How are things?', but will commonly say 'How's things?'. That is, the practice is often very different from the theory. We can draw a parallel here between religious doctrine (the equivalent of langue) and what is actually done in the name of religion (parole). So, the doctrine may speak of peace and compassion, but what can happen in practice can be, by contrast, violence, hate and cruelty. The problem, then, is not so much the doctrine as the implementation of it in a particular cultural, social or political context.

If we want to understand religion, in both its positive and negative aspects, we therefore need to consider the wider context – that is, look at it from a sociological perspective, something that the new atheists clearly failed to do (Figure 22.1).

Armstrong (2010) echoes the significance of the need for a sociological understanding when she argues that:

> Unlike Feuerbach, Marx, Ingersoll or Mill, these new atheists show little concern about the poverty, injustice and humiliation that has inspired many of the atrocities they deplore; they show no yearning for a better world. Nor, like Nietzsche, Sartre or Camus, do they compel their readers to face up to the pointlessness and futility that ensue when people lack the resources to create a sense of meaning. They do not appear to consider the effects of such nihilism on people who do not have privileged lives and absorbing work.
>
> (pp. 293–4)

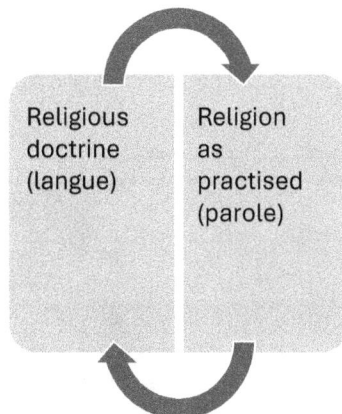

Figure 22.1 Langue and parole

Whether or not we subscribe to a religious faith, it remains the case that presenting a partial view of religion results in a distorted and misleading picture that does not do justice to the complexities involved.

We shall return to the importance of the relationship between theory and practice in the next chapter.

Addressing religion in practice

We have consistently adopted the view that our role is neither to promote religion, nor to attack it. Rather, it is a matter of highlighting the need for a well-considered, well-informed approach when dealing with people in the people professions in circumstances where their religion is a significant factor.

Neglecting a person's or family's religion can give us a less than adequate understanding of important issues in the situation we are seeking to address. It can also create unnecessary barriers. By contrast, respecting a person's religion can build trust and instil confidence and therefore prove empowering.

Exercise 22

How might you show respect for a person's religion? What concrete steps might you be able to take, even if you are not very familiar with the religion concerned?

Making a difference

Introduction to Part III

As this is a *practice* manual, then by definition the emphasis is on practice throughout. So, when we have been discussing theoretical issues, we have been doing so not for their own sake, but as foundations of understanding to cast light on practice issues. But, in this third and final part of the manual, we focus specifically on a number of direct practice issues, organized around a number of themes, with each theme occupying its own chapter.

Here, then, you will discover what we have to say about such important issues as: the importance of perspectives; the loss of meaning and the meaning of loss; forgiveness; social justice; strengths and resilience; celebrating diversity; anti-discriminatory practice; and mental health.

But first, we want to say a few words about the relationship between theory and practice so that there is greater clarity about how we expect your practice to benefit from the discussions in this part of the manual (and, indeed, throughout the manual as a whole).

DOI: 10.4324/9781003682318-26

CHAPTER 23

Relating theory to practice

Introduction

So far, the issues of religion and spirituality have been discussed and put into context. It was acknowledged that religion in particular can be both a positive and negative influence upon people's lives, and the implications of this important insight will be explored in more detail later when we look at anti-discriminatory practice. First, though, we will be exploring some of the ways in which religion and spirituality have a significant impact on practice.

From the outset we need to acknowledge that there are two dimensions to this: the practitioner, and the person who uses the services we offer. Each of us, whether as service providers or service recipients – or at times both – will locate ourselves somewhere on what we might for the sake of convenience call the 'spirituality spectrum'. At one end, there will be those for whom there is a clear overlap between religion and spirituality through their active participation in a faith community. This will very clearly also establish a value base they seek to respect and live by. At the other extreme, there will be those for whom the concept of spirituality, even as defined in this manual as 'what we do to give expression to our chosen worldview', does not sit easily in their thinking, or perhaps even provokes a hostile reaction, for whatever reason. And there will be as many points along this 'spirituality spectrum' as there are people to fill them.

It will be important to focus on both the service provider as well as those who rely on people professionals for support, although it must be admitted that the more familiar approach will be the latter. In other words, professionals like doctors, nurses, social workers, health workers are familiar with the official documentation that may ask for details of a person's religion. In some instances, this will trigger off, perfectly appropriately, a referral to a leader of a faith community whose task will be to explore that person's religious and spiritual needs. Hospital

DOI: 10.4324/9781003682318-27

care is a classic example of this, where a lot of work has been done to help staff recognize the importance of religious and spiritual care, especially in patients whose circumstances give rise to serious concern.

The temptation here, of course, is to regard such issues in a compartmentalized way and to make the assumption that, once a referral has been made, the matter has been dealt with – for example:

- This patient needs a special diet – it's up to the catering manager to provide it.
- This young person needs an interview for a job – the local youth service will sort that out.
- This person needs to learn IT skills – there is a course provided locally that will see to that, and it is free – so that is a double bonus that makes us all feel even better about it!
- This person I am counselling seems to have a link with a local faith community, so that lets me off the hook when it comes to talking about such things that I don't know much about anyway.
- I have ticked the box and made a referral to a leader of a faith community, so that is sorted.
- The person has said 'none' to the question about religious affiliation on my form, so we can forget all about that and get on with the real work.

In other words, there is no point in having a theoretical understanding of spirituality and religion if we do not actually use it in practice in a meaningful way.

Of course, it is wholly appropriate that we recognize the role of chaplains and faith-community leaders in our multi-faith society. They have relevant expertise, and are comfortable in offering religious and spiritual care, often beyond the boundaries of their own particular faith community. But, to restrict religion and spirituality to a narrow box of ecclesiastical conformism is to miss an important point. Muslims are not alone in claiming that their faith is about the whole of life, and that what they believe permeates every aspect of their living. If our definition of spirituality rings true, then we should expect that this permeation will occur to a greater or lesser extent with everybody, even if it is not clearly articulated and regardless of whether they have religious beliefs or affiliations. The worldview and the values a person chooses to live by illustrate the 'heart and soul' of that person – their 'very being' as some would say – and to operate as people professionals in any field without acknowledging that is to diminish the holistic service that many professionals seek to offer.

This is not to suggest that any one person should attempt to be omnicompetent, of course. It is no service to the patient to expect an ear, nose and throat specialist to have a stab at complex brain surgery. There is a vital role for religious leaders to play in caring for people and in dealing with faith and worship issues, and those not trained or familiar with these areas would be doing a disservice to people if they tried to fulfil such a role. The point being made here, however, is not to undermine the role of the faith specialist (if we may use that term), but to stress that such issues can so permeate a person's approach to life that we will be doing them an equal disservice if we do not find ways of exploring these issues with them as far as they relate to the service we are seeking to provide.

But we are in danger already of ignoring one major dimension. It is easy to slip into a discussion (as indeed we have just done) about the needs of patients and people who use the services we offer, and to think that somehow, by virtue of being professional, these issues do not concern us. There is a temptation, in other words, to ignore our own spirituality and the impact it has upon our professional work. And, for those who have a particular allegiance to a faith community and who seek to live by the values inculcated by that allegiance, there may also be particular issues that need to be explored from their professional perspective. This is an important area we will return to in the next chapter.

Key point

Our professionalism requires us to make use of knowledge in practice. Having the knowledge is not enough on its own if it is not playing a part in shaping, for example, our decision making.

Theorizing practice

The traditional way of addressing the relationship between theory and practice is to talk in terms of 'applying theory to practice', which involves beginning with theory and trying to somehow fit it into practice. Thompson (2017) has proposed an alternative approach that better fits the reality of what actually happens in concrete practice situations. He introduces the notion of 'theorizing practice' which involves beginning with practice and then drawing on theory – our professional knowledge base – to make sense of the situation. This avoids trying to fit the square peg of theory into the round hole of practice and, in its place, involves a process of using knowledge that is specific to the particular circumstances.

What this means in terms of religion and spirituality is that, in each practice situation we find ourselves in, we need to be asking ourselves: what does my professional knowledge base tell me about circumstances like this? What do I know about religion and spirituality more broadly that will help me understand this situation and make me better equipped to deal with it?

Exercise 23

What difference do you feel it makes to theorize practice (that is, begin with practice and draw on theory as appropriate) rather than apply theory to practice (that is, begin with theory and try to make it fit the practice situation)?

CHAPTER 24

Perspectives

Introduction

'Me? A spiritual person? You must be joking!' This perhaps all-too-familiar retort not only illustrates the well-used maxim of the subjects to avoid talking about at dinner parties, but also points up the problems of definitions we explored in Part I. Many people lump religion and spirituality together into one untidy heap and, perhaps because of its very untidiness, dismiss it from any serious consideration. The secularization of contemporary British society perhaps lends itself to this reaction. Religion (with its travelling companion, spirituality) is perceived as being pre-Enlightenment or the territory of the fundamentalist zealot. On both counts, many would argue, they deserve to be dismissed.

Consequently, one major task this manual seeks to address is to encourage people to explore a wider definition, such as the one we have suggested, and to see that this is an issue that affects each and every one of us, and is not something we can relegate to the strange fascination of a minority. We would also argue that the values that derive from our chosen worldview – be they specifically religious, atheistic or less clearly defined – are with us in our professional lives as well as in our private lives and need to be acknowledged.

In some ways, this should not be such strange territory as some may think. In the core training curricula for several professions, for example, it is expected that students will be able to develop the skills of reflective practice as part of their educational and professional development. This involves not only the skills of being able to draw on the core underpinning knowledge in practice situations with a developing level of competence but also some other dimensions as well. As we have indicated, the concept of 'self-location' is of particular importance here. Put at its simplest, this means that each of us needs to take into account the

DOI: 10.4324/9781003682318-28

effect of our race/ethnicity, gender, class, disability and so on upon our professional practice and how we relate to the people who come to us for help.

To illustrate the point from the standpoint of sociology, we can gain an insight from what is often called a 'feminist' approach to social research. This has involved a critique of 'malestream' research that is seen as being based upon sexist and patriarchal principles and often excludes the reality of women's experience (Perez, 2019). In other words, whether consciously or unconsciously, men had been allowing their assumptions about women to influence how they had conducted and interpreted their research. It needed women to begin to articulate, and then carry out, feminist research in order to capture or do justice to the richness and variety of women's experience. The point being made is clear: research is not gender neutral.

An anecdote from practice provides a further example. Several years ago, a male social worker was conducting an assessment with a woman and her children who had escaped from serious and prolonged domestic violence and were living in a women's refuge. It became clear after a while that the male social worker's value base and personal cultural worldview emphasized the importance of the family staying together at all costs, and this was reflected in his court report recommendations. Fortunately, the woman's barrister was able to challenge the report and managed to achieve an outcome that fully protected her and the children. The point of the story is clear: although the professional value base of social work stresses the importance of an even-handed assessment that (in this case) needed to recognize the children's interests and safety being of paramount importance, the male social worker's own value base had been allowed to influence the outcome of the report in an inappropriate way.

In case you think that this was an extreme example, it is worth listing some further examples from practice that illustrate the point. As you read through this list, be aware of your own feelings and opinions about the scenarios being suggested. Your reactions will highlight for you something about your own value base and worldview:

- You are a nurse in a hospice and have to offer physical nursing care to someone with HIV/AIDS.
- You are a youth worker and are aware of young people moving from soft to hard drugs and who want you to help them find work.
- You are a care worker in a residential unit for 'looked-after children' and are aware that several of the young people are having sex under the legal age of consent.
- You are working with two people who have learning difficulties who wish to begin a sexual relationship together.
- You work in an area of high unemployment where asylum seekers come to you for help and advice about finding work.
- You have to prepare a court report on a paedophile.
- A female street worker comes to your advice centre for welfare benefits advice.

This small handful of examples has been suggested not to highlight what our professional and legal responsibilities may be – these are often quite clear – but to help us understand that our own values and worldviews are frequently involved in the work we undertake and in the practice dilemmas we face on a regular basis.

Key point

In such complex circumstances there are no definitive 'right answers', but there are plenty of wrong answers, in the sense that if we respond in an insensitive way, we can do a lot of harm.

We can take the matter further, and into the specific realm of religion and spirituality, with a further set of cameos:

- You are a committed member of a faith community and making an assessment about whether or not to recommend a gay couple as potential adopters.
- You work in a medical setting and are faced with cases of male and female circumcision, and wonder if this should be classed as abuse.
- You are the manager of a team where there is a committed Muslim who is claiming the right to have prayer facilities and 'time out' for prayers during the working day.
- You are working with someone who is about to die and appears supremely confident about an afterlife, whereas you are not only unsure but are quite frightened by the thought of dying.
- You belong to a faith community but feel that members of your team consistently devalue you because of your religious beliefs and challenge your capacity to work professionally and not to proselytize.
- You are working with a family who claim that it is culturally and religiously acceptable to exercise physical chastisement upon their children.
- You are working in a hospital setting where a family refuses on religious grounds to allow a blood transfusion to be given to their child.
- You belong to a faith community and are working with someone who is terminally ill. They want to discuss what you think happens after people die.

Again, these cameos are to help you reflect on your attitudes about issues to do with religion and spirituality, and the extent to which your own views differ from, or are similar to, those we have to work with. That is why most of the cameos have not been given a designated role such as a social worker, youth worker, counsellor or nurse, where professional codes of conduct come into play. These cameos are intended to raise our awareness of our personal worldview, our own spirituality and values. In other words, our response tells us something about our own spirituality.

There are of course serious limitations to such an approach. In the professional contexts within which we work there are often clear guidelines, policies and procedures that we are required to follow that may help to alleviate some of the dilemmas we may face. But underlying all of this is the personal professional relationship we strike up with those who come to use the services we offer. Best practice suggests that we do not hide behind the paperwork, however vital the documentation happens to be. Best practice talks about a quality of professional relationship that has an honesty and integrity about it, and which values and respects the dignity of each individual, and the worldview they have chosen. Within the limits of professional codes of practice, we owe it to those who use the services we offer to be as fully human as we can. And that involves unavoidably – but potentially creatively – our own spirituality; for we too need to be able to make sense and give meaning to the world as we experience it, and as we contribute to its wellbeing.

Paradoxically, perhaps, the best way of ensuring that we do provide a complete holistic service to people that takes into account issues of religion and spirituality is to be honest with ourselves about where we are coming from. If we as workers can appropriately locate ourselves in matters to do with religion and spirituality, it will not only help us to keep these issues 'on the agenda', but also ensure that we begin to do justice to the other person's experience.

TIP! A helpful way of developing this sort of self-awareness is to ask yourself from time to time: How are other people seeing me? How am I coming across to them? Am I helping or hindering?

Working with others

We need to bear in mind that these issues of religion and spirituality are not simply a matter of personal whim or enthusiasm: they belong in the mainstream of practice, and we owe it to the people we work with to deal with these matters appropriately.

When it comes to exploring exactly how this might happen, we are faced with a variety of possible approaches that could be adopted in this chapter. We could, for example, simply itemize a large number of scenarios across several professions where religion and spirituality might be legitimately raised and discussed. You could then select the scenarios that seemed to be of greatest interest. Or, we could adopt an approach that selects certain religious and spiritual perspectives, and use these as templates to hold across a range of work-based scenarios to highlight particular issues. We could look at issues from a Christian or Muslim or atheistic point of view, for example, to illustrate how these issues might work in practice.

Each of these approaches could enrich our understanding and practice across a range of disciplines. For present purposes, however, a more modest approach has been adopted whereby some key themes have been identified that span most if not all the disciplines that will be interested in this topic. With each theme an attempt is made in an introductory way to explore the links with religion and spirituality to encourage you to see the possible connections and where these issues have particular relevance. The discussion is not exhaustive but illustrative: a 'starter for ten', rather than a definitive conclusion.

The three main themes chosen for this discussion are:

1. The loss of meaning and the meaning of loss;
2. Forgiveness; and
3. Social justice.

These form the basis of the next three chapters.

Exercise 24

Think carefully about how your own perspective on religion and spirituality affects your work and your approach to it. Refer back to the dilemmas listed above and work out what your own reaction would be. What can you learn about yourself from doing this?

CHAPTER 25

The loss of meaning and the meaning of loss

Introduction

The 'snappy' title for this chapter brings us face to face with an aspect of life that is far from snappy. Loss is, without doubt, one of the biggest themes of human existence and penetrates the work of people professionals at every turn. It would be comforting perhaps to be able to say that, just because it is such a mainstream feature of human living, we have developed robust practical and emotional strategies for dealing with such issues when they arise. But we all know that many of us haven't!

Behind all the labels we wear, the gut-wrenching heartache of real loss hits us all and knocks us sideways. The university professor and the newest student; the NHS consultant and the anxious patient; the nursing sister and youngest recruit; the hospital porter and the person being pushed along on the trolley; the dynamic youth worker and the painfully insecure young person; the experienced counsellor and the person struggling to express their feelings; the manager floundering to support a bereaved worker and the employee trying to get their work done after experiencing a shattering loss; the social worker who 'has seen it all' and the client who is having to 'live it all'; the faith community leader and the person coming for spiritual guidance; the debt adviser and the person with a sackful of unpaid bills – each and every one of us, wherever we find ourselves in the complex tapestry of our community, is likely to feel devastated when experiencing profound loss. However well prepared we think we may be, it seems to be the case that even the best preparations we make can only be at best a moderately strong sea wall that ultimately the crashing waves will breach.

This is not meant to sound gloomy and pessimistic. It is meant to be honest and realistic. And, more importantly, it is intended to express something profoundly significant about being human that puts us in touch with the whole issue of spirituality and what gives meaning and purpose to our lives. It is precisely because we

DOI: 10.4324/9781003682318-29

have the capacity to love that the loss of a loved one hurts so much. Gibran (1926) caught this in his meditation on sorrow and joy: 'When you are sorrowful, look again into your heart, and you shall see that in truth you are weeping for that which has been your delight' (p. 36). Arthur Quiller Couch (1923) caught something of the reality of this when he described grief as: "The unwelcome lodger that squats on the hearth between us and the fire, and will not move or be dislodged'. It is not surprising that literary references start tumbling over each other when this theme is mentioned: its sheer universality strikes a chord in us all.

The significance for our discussion lies not just in the sharp experiences of bereavement, but in the all-embracing domain of loss. Whether it is in the loss of identity and self-confidence; the loss of employment or of a partner through separation or divorce; the loss of physical capacity or mental acuity; or the loss of opportunity through a particular 'failure' – loss strikes at us all. It is no wonder that it is precisely at these times that our sense of meaning, purpose and direction can also take a battering, especially if it was a bit shaky before.

How often in the news bulletins that accompany major disasters do we hear newscasters commenting that 'the people involved are struggling to come to terms with what has happened to them'? The greater the loss, the harder this challenge will feel, and it must be openly acknowledged that, for many people, the gaping chasm left in their lives by a major trauma may never be filled. They may spend the rest of their lives learning how to walk round it with a hesitating familiarity, but the gaping void will never be filled. Anniversaries tear the scab off the emotional wounds; familiar music brings memories flooding back. The walk past the place where you used to work rekindles the ache if not always the anger. Seeing your children happily settled with a new partner brings pangs of guilt about the parenting you can no longer fully provide. Like Gruyere cheese or the pitted lunar landscape, the painful holes become part of our personality whether we like it or not, and the big question hits us: 'What sense can we make of this to enable us to carry on with our lives with some modicum of success and enjoyment?' Or, as Morgan (1983) puts it: 'how can you make sense out of a world that does not seem to be intrinsically reasonable?' (p. 6).

It is at this point that people professionals perfectly reasonably ask for some help from theoretical perspectives and research findings to help them deal with these major issues of loss. In the first instance, they ask this question in order to be better able to provide best practice for those who come to them for help and support. But there is a bonus in this: the theoretical frameworks offer help and encouragement to the worker every bit as much as to those who come to them for professional support. Furthermore, if as workers we can have some real insight into these issues in our own lives, then it is likely that it will increase our sensitivity to those people also experiencing loss we are seeking to work with. And, in terms of the specific topics of this manual, we will find that, perhaps to our surprise, we are in the mainstream of the discussion about spirituality, if not religion itself. For the responses (it's a bit optimistic to expect answers) people give to these profoundly disturbing and challenging questions posed by serious loss are ultimately spiritual, in that they uncover the particular worldview people have chosen to underpin their lives.

It may be, of course, that this chosen worldview proves to be profoundly lacking when the litmus test of deep loss is applied to it. This then increases a person's emotional 'Angst' as they seek to find another worldview that can encompass what their loss has forced them to acknowledge. Painful though the process will be for both the person and the professional helper who may be caught up with them in it all, it need not be viewed in a negative light completely. Crisis intervention theory has taught us to view such 'upheaval moments' as potential opportunities to re-think and re-shape our lives and our priorities (Thompson, 2025b). It provides an opportunity for the person involved and the professionals who are working with them to acknowledge this dimension and not to run away from exploring it, however tempting that might be.

The recent developments in our understanding and appreciation of dealing with loss within the context of bereavement and death-related losses have implications for many other loss experiences. Of the several important theoretical strands to emerge, two in particular deserve mention. The first is meaning reconstruction theory; the second is the 'dual process' model. Both approaches may be seen to have a spiritual dimension to them, although neither of them specifically addresses this perspective in any depth.

Before looking at these two models, however, it is worth saying something about the 'received wisdom' of the 'stages of grief' model that still dominates the theoretical understanding of many people professionals who were brought up on the work of Kübler-Ross and others. It probably says more about those who cling rigidly to the stages model than about those who first offered it as a theoretical approach for understanding grief and loss that it seems to be written in tablets of stone for many practitioners. People are then expected somehow to travel from stage to stage, through shock, denial, anger, bargaining, depression and acceptance (Kübler-Ross, 1969). Helpful though these facets undoubtedly are in shaping our understanding of, and sensitivity to, the experience of loss, the reality for many people is far more complex and multi-layered than such a model would suggest. There is no automatic linear progression through the stages, for example, and the concept of acceptance is far more complex than the word might suggest.

Key point

The stages approach has been very popular for many years, but in fact there is little evidence to support it. In reality, the experience of grief is complex and messy and does not follow any sort of logical pattern of stages.

The following discussion of two recent models is not intended to dismiss all other theories and models 'root and branch', but simply to illustrate how a spiritual dimension can flow naturally and easily from them, and that the topics that they raise have a spiritual dimension.

Meaning reconstruction theory is principally associated with the work of Robert Neimeyer (Neimeyer, 2001, for example). Major loss challenges our 'taken-for-granted' worldview, he argues, so much so that:

> we are faced with the onerous task of revising these taken-for-granted meanings to be adequate to the changed world we now occupy, Simultaneously we must deal with urgent questions about what this loss signifies, whether something of value might be salvaged from the rubble of the framework that once sheltered us, and who we are now in light of the loss or losses sustained. All of this questioning plays out on levels that are practical, existential and spiritual, and all of it is negotiated using a fund of meanings (partially) shared with others, making it as much a social as a personal process.
>
> (Neimeyer and Anderson, 2002, p. 48)

To fully understand this model requires a detailed reading of Neimeyer's own work, but even from this cursory introduction several strands become clear. First of all, there is no time limit upon the process of constructing new meanings. Some may achieve this quickly; for others, it may take years; some may never complete the process. Second, however important other people in our network and cultural group may be, ultimately it is we ourselves who have to make this journey and to make sense of what has happened and is still happening to us. In this regard, the metaphor of a journey may feel very encouraging to many people. A new or revised meaning does not just 'happen': it requires a commitment on our part to help formulate it. Third, the new or revised meaning we construct will not seek to draw a curtain inexorably over the past but will somehow seek to encompass the memories into a present and future framework. Fourth, some losses trigger off an intense need in people to find out about how their loved ones died, especially if this was in the context of a disaster or serious accident. The search for some 'explanations', however impartial, seems to help in the process of moving on and finding meaning for the future. Finally, there seems to be some evidence to suggest that people who are able to look to the future with at least some measure of optimism following a loss will make a better 'fist' of their futures (Franz et al., 2001).

If spirituality is defined as what we do to give expression to our chosen worldview, then the links with meaning reconstruction theory are clear. Serious loss involves at first a 'checking out' of the worldview that had previously sustained us, and if this is then found to be wanting, a process of revision needs to be undertaken in order to make all the pieces of the jigsaw fit together with a reasonable degree of accuracy.

The second model to explore in this context is Stroebe and Schut's (1999) 'dual process' approach to loss and grief. Again, as with previous models, the application to a wide range of losses is important, even though the model was first presented in a framework of bereavement.

Stated simply, this model suggests that a person experiencing loss begins to live in a world where there are two main 'orientations': a loss orientation and a restoration orientation – there is a looking to the past in terms of who and what have been lost and a looking forward to the future, a rebuilding. The crucial aspect of this model is that anyone experiencing a period of severe loss moves in and out of (or 'oscillates' between) these two orientations all the time, often several times in a day or in an hour even. One moment there are floods of tears; the next moment the doorbell rings and a gas meter has to be read, and the matter is handled with appropriate efficiency. One moment there is bleak despair that roots you to the spot with dreadful helplessness; the next moment it is 3 o'clock and you have to fetch the children from school, so you get ready and go out to make sure they are safe. This model suggests that, for as far as the eye can see into our future, we will be moving in and out of these two orientations. As time goes on, we may find ourselves with a greater future focus than we had even dreamed possible; but there will always be those other moments when something triggers a return to the loss orientation and it comes upon us fresh once more.

The key thing is to recognize that our journey 'from here on in' will consist of both aspects, and the way we travel on this journey will be unique to us. No one can tell us in which orientation to be in at any time in order to 'do it properly'. It is 'our call', our journey, and we will, by and large, do it our way (Figure 25.1).

Again, this metaphor of the journey offers help and encouragement both to the person experiencing the loss and to people professionals who may be caught up with them in a helping relationship. Tempting though it may be to tell people how they ought to be feeling, because this or that theory says so, the 'dual process' model puts control back into the hands of the person whose journey it is. The speed at which they travel; the decisions whether or not to pause at certain landmarks, and when (or whether) to go back and revisit them from time to time, are all in the control of the journey maker, not the professional travelling companion. It is in the journey itself – some who are happy with more religious language might prefer to call it a pilgrimage – that new meaning is discovered. And it is probably only if a person comes to rest and gets profoundly 'stuck' in some way that the professional travelling companion needs to act in order to ensure that some skilled 'roadside maintenance' is available to enable the journey to get under way once more.

Within this context, the definition of spirituality as what we do to give expression to our chosen worldview once again has some important things to say. The metaphor of a journey is a very active one, and how people choose to make that journey – the people they choose to travel with; the destinations they pause or stop at; the organizations they join or withdraw from; the causes they support or from now on choose to neglect – all this gives clues as to their worldview, and the

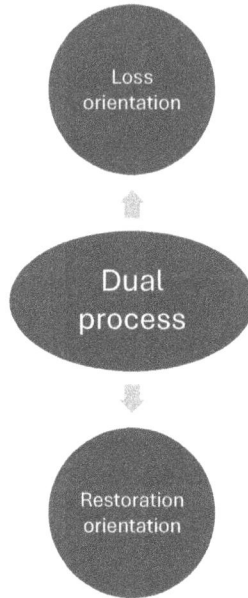

Figure 25.1 The dual process model

extent to which they find it satisfying, emotionally, intellectually and indeed spiritually. These metaphorical landmarks – in the territory of both the loss and restoration orientations – can give their professional travelling companion hints and clues as to what is becoming important for the person they are working with, and how they can best respond in a creative, empathic and creative way.

> **TIP!** When working with people who are deep in the throes of grief, we can feel an intense pressure to try and take their pain away. We need to resist that pressure as it is not possible to do that. The pain is part of the healing. While we can offer solace and reassurance to make the pain easier to bear, we cannot take it away and nor should we try.

There is one final point that needs to be made, and this concerns perhaps the biggest issue of all – the meaning of death itself. It is likely that for many people the issue of death and our mortality raises in the sharpest way the question of meaning.

It makes you think! It puts everything else into perspective!

are but two comments that are often heard in the face of sudden death or times of great tragedy. The big WHY? question is asked, implicitly or explicitly, and not just by those most intimately involved. It is a question that philosophers have grappled with, and one about which most, if not all belief systems – religious or non-religious – have something to say. In some profound way, the answers (if that is the right word) that arise from our particular chosen worldview to the question about the meaning and purpose of life (what is it all about?') are frequently voiced most clearly in the face of death. Here again, this is an issue that is shared across the board, no matter whether we seek to help people in a professional capacity or are on the receiving end of professional help – or both. Scratch any of us deep enough, and somewhere some sort of answer will emerge. Many believe in some sort of 'afterlife', and this gives them both a sense of hope and purpose for their daily living. Many believe that death is the absolute end, and this too shapes their views about how life should be lived. In the context, therefore, of finding or giving meaning to life, the issue of death places the question in its sharpest focus and is perhaps the clearest arena where people professionals need to be aware of, and be able to explore sensitively, issues of religion and spirituality with the people they are seeking to help.

Exercise 25

What do you see as the main challenges of working with someone who is grieving? What have your own experiences of loss taught you about supporting someone through grief?

CHAPTER 26

Forgiveness

Introduction

'Forgive me if I have missed the point here, but ...'

As with many other 'big' words, forgiveness can be used in an almost casual way, as in the example above. It provides an alternative to the lightweight use of the word 'sorry' as we bump into someone in the shopping mall and carry on as if nothing has happened. We offer a mildly apologetic grunt, but nothing more. It certainly does not cost us very much.

By contrast, the heavyweight use of the word, if we may use such a term, is most often associated with religion and faith communities, and with the wayside pulpit posters on display outside church buildings that assail us in traffic jams. Forgiveness is, after all, a religious and theological concept without which most, if not all, faith systems would crumble. It points to the quality of the relationship between the divine Being (however conceived) and individual human 'becomings' whose journey through life is characterized by umpteen failures and shortcomings. Therefore, a constant and continued claiming and accepting of divine forgiveness becomes an essential ingredient for anyone belonging to a faith community. With divine help, individuals can be picked up and dusted down, be encouraged to make a fresh start, and have another 'go' at the complexities of human living. The association of the concept of forgiveness with faith communities and religion is therefore quite clear.

Finding forgiveness

However, from the perspective of people professionals and the range of human issues that confront us on a daily basis, no matter what group of people we work with, there is the important question about whether there is any middle ground

DOI: 10.4324/9781003682318-30

between these two uses of this important word. Can the concept of 'forgiveness' find a place in their working vocabulary? Does it have any relevance? Can it speak to the large number of people who pass the urgent-sounding but often faded roadside posters, and pay not a moment's notice to them precisely because it is 'God talk' and they wish to have nothing whatsoever to do with 'that sort of thing'.

As we noted earlier, one of the difficulties in exploring the theme of religion and spirituality is the search for common ground, and in finding ways in which people's experience can be illuminated and enriched by concepts that previously they had dismissed as irrelevant or not part of 'their scene'. If, however, the context can be reshaped and perhaps become aligned with the concepts of 'change and guilt', then some links may become much more apparent. 'Change' is, after all, at the heart of much of the practice of people professionals, and the experience of feeling guilty about certain aspects of human behaviour is common to a wider range of people who use these services.

The role of guilt
Guilt may be a common enough experience, but it is important to bring some clarity to what is often an ill-defined term. Gordon (2000) suggests that there are three forms of guilt:

(i) Transgression guilt – here the person has actually done something wrong and the feelings of guilt are justifiable and understandable;
(ii) Perfection guilt – comes from falling short of our own or other people's standards and expectations. In other words, the person fails to achieve idealistic standards;
(iii) Rejection guilt – is the product of serious rejection by significant others. This form of guilt stems from 'serious emotional deprivation and verbal and physical abuse. Because the treatment they received was undeserved, the guilt feelings were false'.

(cited in Swinton, 2001, p. 162)

The first two of these definitions can be linked in with our definition of spirituality as what we do to give expression to our chosen worldview. But, before we focus on them, it is worth exploring the third definition in some detail.

Rejection guilt is somewhat different from the first two, in that the worldview in these instances has, in a deep sense, been forced upon someone by abuse. They have been made to feel unclean, dirty, guilty, unworthy and lacking in dignity as a direct result of the abuse they have been forced to experience. In such instances, it is the perpetrator who needs to feel the guilt before any change in behaviour can be achieved. From the victim/survivor perspective, their crucial need is to have their self-respect nurtured back, and to be accepted for the valued person they are in their own right. Any sense of their needing forgiveness would be counterproductive; it would suggest that somehow they are to blame for the abuse they have undergone. If anything, it would increase the burden forced onto them by the perpetrator.

This is not to say, of course, that the victims/survivors do not experience feelings akin to guilt. Many do. In fact, we know that part of a perpetrator's repertoire is the capacity to make their victims feel that they must take some, perhaps even all, of the blame for the perpetrator's abusive behaviour. The task of people professions could be seen, therefore, in part at least, as being a catalyst in helping to remove the 'sick' worldview that has been forced onto the person who has been abused and helping them reclaim a worldview where they have dignity and 'specialness' simply by being who they are.

It is important to give full weight to this role professionals can fulfil in such situations. It stems from the value base of human dignity, individual worth, self-determination, and the rejection of any abusive behaviour. This value base underpins social work and social care, health care, youth work and advice work and beyond; and although the extent to which these issues may be discussed with a victim/survivor may vary according to the agency involved, the fundamental principle remains. The spiritual dimension of this, of course, takes us to the very heart of what we believe it means to be human, how we should treat each other, and our responsibility to challenge oppressive or abusive behaviour when we encounter it.

Key point

People who have been abused are likely to experience a number of losses, and the grief associated with this will often create a sense of 'pseudo-guilt' – that is, feelings that are very similar to guilt, but with no actual basis of anything to feel guilty about.

The second definition of guilt has a clear resonance with a person's chosen worldview, although here again the extent to which the worldview is consciously chosen by them, or for them by their parents' or by other significant people's treatment of them in their early years, is an important question to bear in mind. Nevertheless, the issue is clear: there are people who set themselves unrealistically high achievement targets, and work to such a stringently perfectionist agenda that they can only fall short. That is the point: as with the myth of Sisyphus who would never be able to reach the summit with his rock-pushing task, so too perfectionists can never quite reach their pinnacles of achievement. For some, of course, this scenario remains a creative challenge that helps them bring the best out of themselves, but for others a sense of guilt for under-achievement can soon take over. Indeed, the question is not whether they will fall short – that is guaranteed – but rather the extent to which they will develop a sense of failure and how heavy will be the subsequent burden of guilt they have imposed upon themselves. The worldview that underpins such behaviour has something to do with how such 'driven' people value themselves. They measure their self-worth against a benchmark of an ultimately unattainable achievement and feel guilty as a result.

Here again, the role of people professionals will vary according to the profession. There may or may not be a need for psychological intervention to help the thwarted guilt-ridden perfectionist reshape their worldview. But they will need somehow to learn how to be easier on themselves, and to begin to realize their intrinsic worth, rather than being controlled by a culture where self-worth has somehow to be earned or deserved. The crucial point is that the suggestion or offer of forgiveness from a third party in such a scenario would only serve to reinforce the very system that is creating the guilt in the first place: 'Come on Sisyphus – next time try just that bit harder and I am sure you will make it to the top'. The implication is that the task is achievable, and if, for any reason, there is failure, it is the fault of the person, not the impossible nature of the task.

Paradoxically, the person at the centre of it all will still need to find a way forward to accepting and even forgiving themselves before any sense of healing or completeness can be achieved. But forgiveness in this sense is less about acknowledging wrongdoing, or an unwillingness to give it 100 per cent effort, and much more about recognizing the need for a somewhat reconfigured worldview.

Such a change would help the person centre stage to be much gentler with themselves and to celebrate their intrinsic value and worth, irrespective of their accomplishments. They could begin to measure themselves by what they have been able to achieve, rather than by what is ultimately impossible to attain.

The first definition of guilt is perhaps more familiar to everyone and is much more likely to feature somewhere in the workloads of most people professionals. In the widest sense, we are all conscious of the times when we make a mess of things; when we 'get hold of the wrong end of the stick' and upset people unnecessarily; when we find ourselves behaving in ways that cause pain to other people; and when we are so caught up with our own agendas that we ignore the legitimate needs of others. When the impact of our behaviour begins to dawn on us, and the repercussions of our actions become clear, it is likely that most people will feel anything from a slight twinge to a powerful attack of guilty feelings. We know then that we have done something wrong. It is what happens next that brings us into the realm of spirituality, and the actions we take as a result of the worldview we hold.

Putting things right

Although there are undoubtedly some people whose life skills seem to be particularly focused on trampling on the lives of other people with a psychopathic disregard for their feelings or ultimate value, for many others the realization of wrongdoing more often engenders a sense of guilt and a question about how things can be put right. The issue of change, in other words, is firmly on the agenda. Their worldview is not comfortable with the amount of hurt or upset they have caused, and so they feel instinctively that they need to do something to put things right. And one of the crucial steps in this process – perhaps even, the first step – is this issue of forgiveness.

Canda et al. (2020) note that:

> Forgiveness of self or others can be an important step in releasing pain and preoccupation with feelings of guilt, shame or anger towards oneself and anger and hostility towards others (Garvin 1998). ... Therapeutic forgiveness does not necessarily include pardoning or excusing an offender (Cunningham, 2012; Loue, 2017). That might or might not be considered appropriate by the injured person. No client should be pressured to do so. Indeed, priority might be on holding the offender accountable, seeking justice, and preventing further acts of harm by the perpetrator.
>
> Therapeutic forgiving is definitely not forgetting or repressing, or denying wrongdoing and culpability of an offender.
>
> (pp. 446–7)

All this suggests that words are not enough, although they are often an important starting point. It is what we do to channel our sorrow at hurting others into some actions that will begin to put things right that really matters.

Examples from the wide range of work undertaken by people professionals easily come to mind. Relationships that begin to falter; children and young people whose behaviour brings them into conflict with parental or authority figures; neighbours in dispute; abusive and exploitative behaviour towards children, young people and/or elders; harassment on the basis of gender, sexuality, disability: the list is endless. And the one thing they all have in common is that such behaviours need to be challenged and changed, because they contravene our values and beliefs and worldviews about how people should be treated and respected.

The process of working with people to effect change is a mainstream activity for many people professionals. Social workers, probation officers and prison officers come most readily to mind, but youth workers, psychologists and advice workers also fulfil this role from time to time. The role forgiveness can play in this process is of great importance and is being increasingly recognized in secular settings as well as in specifically religious contexts.

Several strands can be identified. First, an important step in the process of effecting change is for people to be able to forgive themselves for the occasions on which they have let themselves down by acting in such negative and damaging ways. This has resonances with the recovery regime advocated for those who misuse drugs or alcohol and wish either to reduce their involvement with these substances, or to become 'clean'. The first step in the process is not only to admit that the problem exists, but also to acknowledge that people owe it to themselves to accept that the process of change is worthwhile. As long as they do not think that they are worthy of living a better, more fulfilled life, then change will not happen.

A second stage that is becoming increasingly recognized in the criminal justice system, for example, is the determination to do something to demonstrate that the remorse for the negative or anti-social behaviour is really meant. Reparation schemes and opportunities for offenders to meet with their victims to hear about the impact of their offending behaviour are becoming increasingly popular. When faced with the full consequences of their actions, people may be more likely to put into effect those changes in lifestyle that are necessary to reduce the level of suffering inflicted upon others.

A third stage is perhaps the most significant, when people who have inflicted hurt upon others openly apologize for their actions and ask for the other person's forgiveness. There is nothing automatic in this process: it will 'cost' a lot for the person who is asking for forgiveness, and it will 'cost' the person who has been injured in whatever way, to agree to forgive the person who has hurt them. But if the forgiveness is genuinely requested and willingly granted, then the restoration of the relationship can be at a far deeper and more honest level than before.

From the victim/survivor's perspective, however, the hurt may run so deep that such hope for a reconciliation is neither possible nor appropriate. But this is not to say that in such cases forgiveness is a 'non-starter'. On the contrary, there is likely to come a point where the anger, bitterness and resentment are eating so deeply into their lives that the original hurt is being exacerbated, and the quality of the person's life is even more diminished. In these situations, if the victim/survivor can find a mechanism for letting go of the resentment – be this through a personal act of affirmation, or through a counselling or a religiously based intervention if this is appropriate – then there is a chance that a new future can open up as a result of this act of forgiveness.

Forgiveness and social justice
We tend to think of forgiveness as a micro-level phenomenon, a reflection of interpersonal relationships. However, there is also a macro-level aspect to consider. What we have in mind is the role of truth and reconciliation and reparation initiatives following large-scale injustices. In this way, we can see a link between forgiveness and social justice.

The concept of truth and reconciliation relates to efforts to confront past injustices to achieve some form of collective healing. One example of this would be Truth and Reconciliation Commission (TRC) set up in South Africa following the immense harm arising from the apartheid regime, with its catalogue of human rights violations and oppressive practices on racial grounds. Its aim was to promote forgiveness and collective healing (Gibson, 2006). Truth telling in such processes is geared towards establishing a shared understanding of the past and thereby create opportunities for healing the immense traumas involved

(Clark, 2012). In this way, the TRC was a social justice initiative based on the view that establishing truth and acknowledging grievances and the harm done are a necessary basis for promoting social cohesion and thereby laying the foundations for future positive social relations (James et al., 2020). Another example would be the important work undertaken in Northern Ireland in the aftermath of the 'Troubles' in establishing a basis for harmonious relations across the whole community there.

Reparation is another way of facilitating social forgiveness. It is not simply a matter of establishing financial compensation for wrongs done. It also has a symbolic function of acknowledging such wrongdoings and validating victims' experiences. This, in turn, can promote dignity and thereby improve trust and social cohesion (Chavez et al., 2024) and once again facilitate healing from the traumas involved. An example of such reparation would be the Prime Minister of the Netherlands issuing a formal apology in 2022 on behalf of his government for the country's role in slavery and the transatlantic slave trade in its former colonies and providing financial recompense.

Forgiveness and spirituality

This chapter began with the question of whether some middle ground could be discovered between a casual use of 'forgive' and its 'heavy-duty' religious connotations, in which people professionals could feel 'at home' in the range of work they undertake. The discussion has explored various aspects of guilt, change and forgiveness to demonstrate that such ground does indeed exist. The language used has deliberately avoided any religious or spiritual overtones. although any reader who belongs to a faith community will have quickly made links to those dimensions. But, in the context of our definition of spirituality, there are some important points that deserve to be drawn out.

1. Any acknowledgement of guilt or remorse has a spiritual dimension in that it puts us in touch with our understanding of the sort of people we are or could be. It reminds us of our vulnerability, our capacity to inflict harm as well as to do good, and the feelings this generates within us.
2. It points up the worldview we hold and challenges us to locate our behaviour within a framework that has the capacity to offer some sort of rationale that can encompass our negative actions, as well as the potential for putting things right. Some faith systems are particularly strong in this area, but such frameworks are by no means limited to religious systems.
3. Forgiveness as an activity has a strong value base that respects other people as being intrinsically worthy as individuals. Here again there are strong links with faith systems in this regard.
4. Forgiveness does not carry with it any implication that abuse is anything other than abuse. Any activity that damages other people or severely limits their life chances or quality of life is to be roundly condemned and, if

necessary, subject to the full weight of the law and its penalties. Forgiveness is not 'going soft' but is the opportunity for a courageous new start.

5.   There is nothing automatic about forgiveness. It is costly to request and costly to grant, but if it has a full impact upon all those involved it can transform relationships.

6.   As with any major event that has an impact upon our lives, our worldview needs either to be capable of incorporating such new dimensions, or to be open to challenge, or even to replacement by a more satisfying worldview.

One final point needs to be made. So far, the emphasis of the discussion has been upon individual behaviour, by and large, and this is without doubt a hugely important dimension. But it has wider connotations, as Professor Marc Ellis, the distinguished Jewish theologian, who has been challenging his own people's abuse of the Palestinians, makes clear. He writes that:

> forgiveness could only come within a commitment to justice. 'People cannot simply 'forgive' – invite back into their lives on a mutual basis – those who continue to violate us', one student wrote, 'otherwise "forgiveness" is an empty word. Forgiveness is possible only when the violence stops. Only then can those who have been violated even consider the possibility of actually loving those who once brutalised and battered them. Only then can the former victims empower the victimisers by helping them to realise their own power to live as liberated liberators, people able to see in themselves and others a corporate capacity to shape the future'. It is in the ending of injustice and the journey towards a mutual and just future that forgiveness becomes revolutionary.
>
> (Ellis, 2000, p. 276)

Here a new corporate dimension enters the discussion, and it provides an important link to our third main theme: social justice.

Exercise 26

What possible role do you envisage forgiveness playing in your particular line of work? In what way might this be seen as a spiritual matter?

CHAPTER 27

Social justice

Introduction

There is no doubt that the themes of religion and spirituality are seen by many as being intensely personal, private even. They touch our lives at the deepest level and illuminate what some call the 'core of our being'. They are issues that may be deeply held and intensely felt but are not shared or discussed with others very often. From the people professional's point of view, it may be important to uncover such issues in an attempt to understand how the person who has come for help really 'ticks', but it all still remains at the individual level.

Our definition of spirituality as what we do to give expression to our chosen worldview will not allow it to stop there. Certainly, there is a strong individualistic strand to the definition, but it also has an important social dimension. Our worldviews will clearly need to be intellectually and emotionally satisfying to us individually by giving us some insight into our place within the wider fabric of society and also (for those within certain faith communities) a hope for our ultimate destiny. But a wider understanding of spirituality is called for if this definition is to hold.

Moss explored this dimension in a previous work when he argued that:

> One final dimension needs to be raised, a dimension which has common threads in both faith-community and more general definitions of spirituality. This is the dimension of passion and justice. Alongside very personal and private views of spirituality there are wider perspectives which find expression certainly in the monotheistic traditions. Here we find that a real love of the divine being (however conceived) and a real commitment to

DOI: 10.4324/9781003682318-31

what is required of people of faith, is measured not by the fulsomeness of piety, but by the degree of zeal for truth and justice, in seeing right prevail, captives set free, and the hungry fed.

(Moss, 2002, p. 38)

Here we have an important dimension to this discussion that will perhaps echo the concerns expressed in much contemporary practice that seeks to challenge discrimination and oppression. It is not enough to apply the sticking plaster and bandages on individual wounds if the problems that are causing the pain are more deep seated and societal in nature. Of course, it is essential that individuals receive the care they need and deserve, but if the fundamental causes are not addressed, then the queue for help will simply get longer and longer.

This dimension to religion and spirituality, however, is not widely recognized. And yet the worldviews that are offered by various faith systems do have a component that takes seriously these issues of social justice, because they are intrinsically bound up with the worldview they espouse. It is worth pausing now to give some examples that illustrate this point, albeit very briefly.

Judaism

The story of the Jewish faith is a complex one, with a powerful leitmotif of suffering at the hands of the oppressor. Early experiences of exile and the suffering that was etched upon the nation's soul as a result remains a dominant strand that has only been strengthened by events such as the Holocaust. Alongside these experiences has been the conviction that they have been a chosen people, and that however great the desolation, their God (referred to as Adonay) will not only rescue and liberate them, but will also ultimately vindicate them in the eyes of the world as the channel through which the goodness of Yahweh will stream for the benefit of all (see, for example, Isaiah 60 vv 1–3 in the Hebrew bible).

Fundamental to their life has been the Torah and its commentaries and interpretations in the Talmud that offer both general and, at times, very detailed guidance as to how people should live one with another. In this sense, it is a religion of the book, where the obligations towards family and community are spelled out. The covenant relationship between Adonay and the chosen people needs to be reflected in the ways in which people treat each other with justice (zsedakah, literally righteousness), loyal devotion (hesed, literally kindness), and peace (shalom).

In other words, the worldview of being a people called into being and chosen by Adonay, lays obligations upon its members: an inward-looking self-centredness is simply not part of the package, however pious or spiritual the person may be (Deuteronomy 7 vv 7–8; 9: 4–7).

Alongside this is an important strand where oppressive and discriminatory practices are identified and challenged. This is seen in people called prophets, who acted as the conscience of the nation by reminding them of the full implications of the worldview they shared. In this way, we find Amos challenging the Jewish people with these words:

> You have oppressed the poor and robbed them of their grain... you persecute good people, take bribes and prevent the poor from getting justice in the courts. Make it your aim to do what is right, not what is evil, so that you may live. Then the lord God Almighty really will be with you as you claim he [*sic*] is. Hate what is evil, love what is right and see that justice prevails in the courts... let justice flow like a stream, and righteousness like a river that never runs dry.
>
> (Amos 5 vv 11–24 selected verses. See also Isaiah 35 vv 1–10 and 61 vv 1–4; Micah 6 vv 6–8 in the Hebrew Bible)

The significance of the prophetic strand should not be underestimated for the impact it has had within both Christianity and Islam, and also in more secular manifestations and commitments to social justice. Within Judaism there is also the strong future messianic hope that one day peace between all peoples will reign forever.

Here we find a passion for justice; a sense of outrage that some people were being treated unfairly; a deep yearning for liberation, all located within a worldview that was saying something about how these deep concerns stemmed from an understanding of the nature of the supreme being to whom the Jewish people believed they owed their very existence.

Some more detail has been given in this chapter than in some of the following ones because some of the themes find echoes in later faith systems.

Islam

Much of Islam as a faith system acknowledges the debt it owes to both Judaism and Christianity and respects their moral teachings and writings. Righteousness and justice are upheld as core values, and stem from an obedience and submission to Allah. As in Judaism, so too with Islam, there is a central corpus of influential writings, principally the Qur'an – the revealed word of Allah in Arabic given to the prophet Mohammed (p.b.u.h. = peace be upon him) whose example is contained in the Sharia, 'the way' or the law.

Some key injunctions to lead a holy and upright life, where justice is at the centre, are expressed in Chapter 2 v 110; 148; 177; 215, and in Chapter 4 v 135 that says:

> Establish justice (al-qist) being witnesses for God – even if the evidence goes against yourselves or against your parents and kinsmen; and irrespective of whether the witness is rich or poor; under all circumstances God has priority.
>
> (cited in Thakur, 1996, p. 39)

Alongside this are the injunctions to give to charity and to cultivate a generous disposition towards others. There is also within some aspects of Islam the future hope that injustice, oppression and tyranny will be swept away by Allah, and a true harmony established for all who live in obedience to the will of Allah.

Again, the worldview is important. Muslims believe that issues of human justice are of concern to them precisely because it is a concern of Allah, and that the essential obedience to Allah that is at the heart of the faith brings with it a concern for social justice.

Hinduism

Although a different kind of faith system from the monotheism of Judaism and Islam (and also Christianity), Hinduism has a strong sense of cosmic order that is to be reflected in those who subscribe to its worldview. This is based on Rig Veda, one of the four main sacred writings of Hinduism (the Vedas). Here there is an emphasis upon the idea of 'dharma' that stands for the 'cosmic order, the law, justice, morality and the very fabric of social order' (Thakur, 1996, p. 29). Within Hinduism there is the notion that the deeds in this life will influence the quality and type of living experienced in the next life, for good or ill (karma). This provides a strong encouragement for people to live a life where the needs of others are taken into account. There is also the hope for a golden age of justice, peace and plenty, although unlike other faith systems this golden age will not necessarily be at the end: it too may crumble and fade away in the endless cycle. There is nevertheless a strong emphasis upon the virtues of justice and right dealing between people, enshrined most famously in the life and work of Mahatma Gandhi and his tireless work for the non-violent liberation of his people.

Atheism and humanism

It is important to recognize that, for many people, there is as deep a spirituality within the bundle of beliefs that constitute an atheistic or humanist worldview, as in any of the faith systems others subscribe to. It is probably less appropriate to talk of doctrines in this context, as that term has religious connotations that many atheists and humanists would clearly reject. Nevertheless, many of the contributions to art, music and culture, as well as politics, are made by people who have no religious affiliations, but who nevertheless would acknowledge and own a spiritual dimension to their lives, in the way in which they view and value the natural world and their responsibilities to other human beings. Whether they work through organized politics or through pressure groups or interest groups, there is a clear commitment to social justice and the improvement of the quality of life for others.

Unlike faith communities, there is a less identifiable 'clubbable quality' among atheists or humanists, partly because their chosen worldview does not require it in the same way as a religious faith system would, and partly because there are not so many common denominators as in an organization that people consciously choose to join. This is not to say, of course, that everyone who espouses this worldview would believe the same things or engage in similar activities – far from it – but for present purposes it is important to recognize that the passion for justice that is an important dimension to spirituality has taken root in the lives of many people who have no religious allegiance, but whose commitment to the betterment of the social order burns as fiercely and as brightly as anyone else's.

Christianity

Many of the points already made in connection with Judaism and Islam hold true for Christianity, which was born in the same Middle Eastern cradle. It shares with Judaism some of the same passion for justice and obedience to the will of God. It shares with Islam the significant influence of its founder, although the claims for the person of Christ far exceed those made in later generations for Mohammed. Christ's teachings around the theme of social justice are based on the notions of loving one's neighbour, refusing to take revenge and being willing to forgive without limit. A further dimension to Christ's teachings is on the idea of the Kingdom of God. These are couched in such everyday language that it is reasonable to imply that they were standards he felt people could not only aspire to but also attain in their relationships one with the other.

A prophetic strand in the teaching also challenged the religious authorities of the day for their neglect of justice. Parables such as the Good Samaritan (Luke 10 w 25–37) and the great judgement between the sheep and the goats (Matthew 25 w 31–46) have immense power precisely because the acid test of faithfulness was whether people cared for the wounded, fed the hungry, clothed the poor and visited the sick (see too Luke 1 w 46–55 that still reads like a political manifesto of what the world could look like).

Once more the same point needs to be made: the worldview that claims that everything owes its existence to the creative power of God makes demands of its followers to mirror in their own lives the living and forgiving nature of God that they have been invited to enjoy through Christ.

These snapshots (and they are nothing more than that) into a number of worldviews have illustrated the central theme of this chapter. Religion and spirituality are to be seen in a context much wider than individual and self-centred interest. There is within many of these worldviews, religious and secular, a burning passion for justice and the improvement of living conditions for the people who inhabit this planet. As Brandon (2000) notes: 'The spiritual road is about living out our uniqueness, not our individualism' (p. 17).

This concern for justice can be summarized as follows:

> In this passionate conviction that all deserve equality of treatment and respect, there is an underlying passionate spirituality that has an energy and a restlessness that will not find peace until truth and justice prevail.

Maybe if more of this spirituality had been in evidence in recent decades, some of the antipathy between social work, as just one of the human services for example, and spirituality might have been avoided.

(Moss, 2002, p. 38)

This review of some of the more political and social justice dimensions to spirituality has tried to make clear the strong links that could exist between people professionals and the great themes of religion and spirituality. However much people professionals are caught up in the everyday needs of individuals who come to them for help, advice or treatment, there is always the wider dimension that underpins their work. Anti-discriminatory practice alerts us to the importance of wider issues of social justice (Thompson, 2021a). It is not good enough to assume that all problems are the fault of the individual, and to seek to pathologize each and every condition we encounter. There are some wider forces at work that we need to take into account.

Key point

Despite the tendency to think about religion and spirituality in individualistic terms, there are many sociological dimensions to such matters, particularly when it comes to issues relating to social justice.

Practice implications

■ Advice workers spend a huge amount of time with individuals who are overwhelmed by mountains of debt, or who are not receiving the benefits to which they are entitled. Organizations such as Citizens' Advice therefore have a social policy dimension to their work. This seeks deliberately to understand some of the wider issues that are affecting the life chances of people in their communities, so that they can put pressure on government at local and national level to make appropriate changes to the system.

■ Youth and community workers devote much of their energy to working with young people who sometimes have to live with the stigmatizing label 'disaffected'. Often excluded from education, their life chances seem to be dwindling. Workers will spend a lot of time trying to open doors for young people and to motivate them to find satisfying jobs and careers. But, unless something structural is done to recognize and address some of the issues that are causing the 'disaffection', the difficulties will remain.

■ Social workers, probation officers and prison officers spend a lot of time with a wide range of people who use their services, across all ages and conditions, and

■ frequently encounter ways in which the odds are stacked against certain groups in society – for example, older people; people with mental health problems; disabled people; black and Asian people; LGTBQ+ people. Many of these groups still do not feel they are living in a society where equality of opportunity is possible. Although in some ways these people professionals, as employees, have limited opportunity for challenging the status quo, the importance of using various channels to highlight major societal concerns cannot be underestimated.

- Health care workers invest considerable time and energy into individual issues of health care but have a much stronger record than others for initiating research into both community health and individual conditions in order to improve the life chances of those who come to them for help and treatment.

- Managers will be called upon to assist individual staff members in difficulties (due to stress, for example), but a wider understanding of where the problems are coming from places them in a much stronger position.

In all these examples, there is an underlying passion for, and commitment to, social justice by seeking to point up the oppressive discriminatory issues that limit individual life chances, and to conduct research in order to find ways of enhancing the quality of life for individuals and society as a whole. Here, surely, a secular spirituality is at work.

In this chapter there have been several mentions of discrimination and oppression and so we now turn to the wider area of anti-discriminatory practice in the context of religion and spirituality, focusing over the next three chapters on strengths and resilience, embracing diversity and anti-discriminatory practice.

Exercise 27

Think back to the earlier discussion of the parallel between langue and parole in linguistics and the differences between how religion is intended and how it works out in practice. In what ways might the positive liberatory potential of religion be capitalized upon in your work and how can you address the discrimination that can also arise from religious beliefs?

CHAPTER 28

Strengths and resilience

Introducing a strengths perspective

Considerable emphasis has been placed in this manual upon the importance and impact of the worldviews people hold. Our working definition of spirituality suggests that it is what we do to give expression to our chosen worldview. If we see the world in a certain way, then it follows that we will seek to behave in ways that express that worldview. This definition carries with it, of course, the possibility of both negative and positive outcomes. Just as religion has at times been experienced as a negative force in people's lives, so too with spirituality. If a person's worldview is based on a paradigm of abuse and leads to abusive behaviour, then that has to be challenged, and vulnerable people have to be protected. The underpinning value base of respect, dignity and intrinsic worth of each individual provides a litmus test for people's spirituality, just as much as any other human activity. If someone's spirituality does not in some sense, directly or indirectly, contribute to the enrichment of humanity, then it stands condemned, or at the very least 'sidelined' as narcissistic self-indulgence.

How people professionals view the people they are required to work with is of fundamental importance, not least because it will influence the way they treat them. The advice worker who regards asylum seekers as potential scroungers is likely to find it difficult to accord to them the dignity and respect that are their right as human beings. Nurses who have strong anti-abortion views are likely to find it difficult to treat with care and respect a young woman who comes to them for a second or third termination. Youth workers who regard 'disaffected' young people as lazy and workshy are going to find it difficult to show them respect and to work with them creatively, social workers who view older people as helpless and unable to cope are unlikely to see them as resourceful people who may not necessarily need to be 'shunted off' to a home where everything is done for them.

DOI: 10.4324/9781003682318-32

133

Probation officers and prison staff who have themselves been burgled or had their car stolen may find their professionalism challenged when working with people who have committed such offences. Managers under considerable pressure themselves may struggle at times to appreciate the pressures that are contributing to a staff member's less than wonderful level of performance.

The examples are endless, but the point is clear: our values affect our behaviour, and how we view the world and other people is of fundamental importance to the sort of people we are and how we treat others.

There is one area of particular importance that deserves attention that arises directly from the worldview we have as professionals. This concerns the extent to which we see the people who come to us as being 'problems' or as people who have strengths and potential that can be utilized in tackling the difficulties that currently face them.

If we are honest, many people professionals work with a 'deficit model' in their everyday practice. In other words, they make a basic set of assumptions about the people they work with that involves a degree of labelling. It goes something like this:

> We (the professional workers/managers) are strong, capable, insightful, well trained, resourceful, able to solve problems, and to be successful helpers. You (the service user/client/employee), by contrast, are weak, unable to solve your problems, lacking insight, somewhat helpless, and therefore so fortunate to have us to work with you to give you the benefit of our skills and knowledge, so that some measure of improvement can be achieved in your mediocre lives.

This somewhat overstated caricature is likely to ring bells with people professionals precisely because so much professional training and practice is often implicitly based upon the model that 'the professional knows best'. Without doubt, such a model has its place, particularly when it comes to legal or medical expertise. But elsewhere there are dangers in refusing to see that everyone has strengths and potential that can be encouraged and utilized in tackling difficulties and problems.

Therefore, the first challenge is precisely this: to what extent do we as professionals have a worldview that recognizes and celebrates the strengths other people have, including those who come 'for help'? Is 'help' something we as workers have in an abundant supply and which we then dispense to others less fortunate than ourselves; or is 'help' something that is intrinsically present within every person, but which may need someone else sometimes to release it within us?

The concept of a 'strengths perspective' is becoming increasingly important in the people professions. As Hodge (2003) noted:

> This framework posits clients' personal and environmental strengths as central to the helping process... without a reliable means for finding

clients' strengths, practitioners tend to revert to practice models that are based upon the identification of problems and deficits.

(p. 14)

Not for the first time the challenge comes to people professionals, and raises questions about their own spirituality, their own worldview and what they do to give expression to it. The professional challenge is to take seriously the concept of 'partnership working' which now occupies a central place certainly within both the literature and practice. Perhaps the new challenge facing us, however, is not just to recognize a 'strengths perspective', but also to acknowledge that spirituality and the issues surrounding it are not the prerogative of the professional helpers but are intrinsic to the human condition, whether or not they are openly acknowledged. One of the strengths to be explored for everyone, therefore, is the sense of what gives meaning and purpose to living, and how that can be enhanced and strengthened.

The central point being stressed here from a practice perspective is the importance of recognizing a 'strengths perspective' and the contribution spirituality, and sometimes religion, can make to the people we work with. We need to recognize that we will be doing them a disservice if we neglect such issues. It is time that 'best practice' openly acknowledged the importance of these issues for all professionals.

Alongside the 'strengths perspective' is another theme that deserves to be explored in the context of spirituality and religion and that is the concept of 'resilience'. Resilience theory has a contribution to make in its own right to our understanding of children and young people. From our perspective, however, there seem to be important insights into the contribution that religion and spirituality can make to people's lives that may give a new direction to this important theoretical perspective.

New directions in resilience theory

The contribution of resilience theory to our understanding of how children and young people cope with, and survive, experiences of great hurt and disadvantage has already been noted. Indeed, there is an increasing literature on this important subject and its implications to help us understand the phenomenon of overcoming stress or adversity (Thompson and Cox, 2020). This is a complex issue, where a number of factors influence the outcome. For example, Rutter (1999) found, in his exploration of resilience theory and its impact upon family therapy, that:

The psychopathological effects of risk experiences are strongly moderated by how individuals cognitively and affectively process their experiences and how the resulting working model of relationships is integrated into their self-concept

(p. 139)

This seems to have close parallels with some of the issues being raised in this manual. What Rutter seems to be suggesting, in effect, is that the child or young person is faced with the challenge of either incorporating their experience and understanding of adversity into their existing worldview or, alternatively, to reshape their worldview in order to bring about a more comprehensive understanding. The more capable someone is of achieving this, the more resilient they are likely to be in the face of such adversity. Rutter argues that:

> For psychologically healthy adult development and relationships, people need to accept the… reality of the bad experiences they have had, and to find a way of incorporating the reality of these experiences into their own self-concept, but doing so in a way that builds on the positive while not denying the negative.
>
> (p. 135)

This has clear parallels with the discussions earlier about the ways in which people's chosen worldviews are, or are not, capable of incorporating new sets of experiences into a deeper understanding. Interestingly, it also has close parallels with Neimeyer's 'meaning reconstruction' theory that is making such an impact upon our understanding of the ways in which people reshape their worldviews in the aftermath of significant loss, as we discussed earlier.

TIP! Beware of falling into the common trap of seeing resilience in narrow individualistic terms. Where people struggle to be resilient, it is not simply a character flaw or inadequacy on their part. Much will depend on the wider context – how much support and encouragement they have had or what access to resources they may have, for example.

The contribution resilience theory has made to our understanding of children's and young people's experiences of adversity seems capable of a wider application. Indeed, the whole concept of resilience seems to offer an important dimension to many of the issues being raised in this manual.

Many people, for example, who belong to faith communities would want to claim that the worldview they have adopted as a result of joining these groups provides an extra dimension that helps them both grapple with, and find intellectually and emotionally satisfying responses to, many of the big issues facing humanity. Those who believe, for example, that there is a further dimension to existence after death, often claim that this faith helps them put the experiences of grief and loss into a framework that helps them make more sense of it all. For such people, their religious faith is an important factor in developing their emotional resilience in the face of death, grief and loss. In a similar way, Muslims (and others) who believe that everything that happens to them has a purpose that ultimately must reflect the will and purpose of Allah, will want to argue that this too increases their emotional resilience and capacity to cope in the face of adversity. For those who belong to faith-based organizations, the love and care and support of others who belong to it provide a major boost to their emotional resilience in times of adversity.

This is not to suggest for one moment that people who do not belong to quite different organizations fail to receive similar levels of resilience-enhancing support from those who also belong to the same group. The point is similar in both cases: it is the acknowledgement that resilience is an important concept and that a crucial question for everyone is to identify what enhances and what reduces this capacity within us. This capacity is especially important in times of difficulty, of course, and one further question to ask is the extent to which the organizations we belong to can make a contribution to this capacity for resilience. The importance of faith-based organizations is that part of their raison d'être is to focus explicitly on some of the very areas of living and dying that most greatly perplex people and to offer a worldview that seeks to locate these painful and problematic experiences within a particular framework.

The same point may be made in connection with the wider issues of spirituality, which, as we have argued, has strong connections with the issues of meaning and purpose, and our chosen worldviews. However people may define spirituality, and whatever activities may flow from their chosen definition, one of the questions that can be legitimately asked is the extent to which that chosen worldview enhances their resilience in the face of adversity.

The links with the core values being discussed in this chapter – especially the capacity to celebrate diversity – are clear. Does a person's, or for that matter an organization's, worldview and value base enhance or diminish people's resilience? If, for example, a particular worldview sees black people, or women, or LGTBQ+ people or disabled people as essentially inferior to other members of the community, then that worldview may be seen as diminishing the resilience of black people, women, LGTBQ+ people and disabled people precisely because of the limitations and restrictions it imposes upon those groups of people. By contrast, a worldview that celebrates diversity and welcomes the enrichment that everybody can make to the community as a whole can be seen to be enhancing resilience precisely because it values everyone's contribution.

It may be tempting to conceptualize power as being solely in the hands of the recognizably powerful within government, industry, or various organizations and then to lament the way in which it is wielded, as if power were something foreign to us. There is, of course, some undoubted truth in this certainly, at the macro level of society, but to limit our understanding in such a way is to misunderstand the nature of power that pervades every aspect of human living. The person who sits in stony silence during an interview is exercising immense power, however disconcerting it may feel to the interviewer who is used to 'calling the shots'. One of the seminal theorists in this field, Michel Foucault, saw power as a feature of all social relationships: 'What I am attentive to is the fact that every human relation is to some degree a power relation. We move in a world of perpetual strategic relations' (1988, p. 168, cited in Thompson, 2018b, p. 68).

This has clear links with the discussion about strength perspectives, in that Foucault's analysis encourages all of us, in whatever relationships or roles we are involved, to examine how we use the power we have, and in what ways it operates within our relationships, personal or professional. We each need to explore the impact of the power we exercise and to assess whether it is being used in a positive and creative way, or in a negative, destructive manner. From a practice perspective, we can also earmark this issue as worthy of discussion with the people we serve to share some dialogue with them about how they use power in their relationships and the impact it has on others.

Furthermore, in terms of the issues central to this part of the manual – anti-discriminatory practice, celebrating diversity and the passion for justice at the heart of spirituality – the theme of power is of crucial importance. Power is not just about what we can make happen in a positive way; it is also about what we can stop happening. Power can be used to keep people from their just entitlements, as well as allowing equality of access and opportunity. As Thompson (2018b) observes:

> Power is therefore a central feature of the struggle to promote equality. Indeed, the very term 'struggle' is a significant one, as it indicates that there are established structures and vested interests that are likely to stand in the way of progress. Promoting equality inevitably involves entering into conflict with the 'powers that be', the dominant social arrangements that help to maintain existing power relations. Consequently, we need to recognize that an understanding of the workings of power is an essential part of challenging inequality, discrimination and oppression.
>
> (p. 61)

Inevitably, this discussion needs to take for granted much of the substance of the theoretical debates about power that are explored and critiqued in the literature (see Thompson, 2018b).

This chapter has sought to make some important links between what may be called the secular theoretical frameworks of anti-discriminatory practice within the context of celebrating diversity and the religious, spiritual and theological perspectives on these key issues. The key themes of a strengths perspective, resilience, and an understanding of power have found shared territory which, at the very least, suggests that there may be more allies sharing a common struggle than many had previously suspected. From the people professional's standpoint, however, it has raised the important awareness that religion and spirituality may highlight strengths, resilience and a thirst for social justice in people that mirrors the professional's own commitment to these core values. But this is not necessarily so. As we noted earlier, religion in particular, but also spirituality can have a negative as well as a positive impact, and so we now need to turn to the practical implications of this.

Exercise 28

How could you identify people's strengths? What tools do you have to enable you to do that? And how might you use awareness of such strengths to promote resilience?

CHAPTER 29

Embracing diversity

Introduction

The demands of best practice are often enshrined in codes of practice that set out how workers should behave and what standard of service those who come to them for help should reasonably expect to receive. Underlying such codes of conduct, however, are the core values that the profession or organization holds, and that it seeks to inculcate in all those who have a role to play within it.

One of the core values that underpins this manual is anti-discriminatory practice, a theme that has been widely explored in the literature (see Thompson, 2018b, 2021a, 2021b, for good introductions to this topic). This theme acknowledges that society is structured in such a way that certain members – black people, disabled people, LGTBQ+ people for example – do not get a 'fair crack of the whip'. They are systematically discriminated against in all manner of ways, and it is the responsibility of people professionals to understand that, and to work in such a way as to counteract, wherever possible, the oppressive impact of that discrimination upon the person coming to them for help.

For Thompson it is crucially important to recognize the interweaving of the personal, cultural and structural aspects of discrimination, often referred to as PCS analysis, rather than viewing it in a narrow legalistic sense.

> **Key point**
>
> It is essential to recognize that seeing discrimination in narrow, individualized terms as personal prejudice provides a limited and distorted view. To get a fuller, more adequate view, we must also take account of cultural and structural factors and how all three levels – personal, cultural and structural – interact and reinforce one another.

DOI: 10.4324/9781003682318-33

What we are dealing with here takes us immediately into the earlier discussion about worldviews and the ways in which people's behaviour is affected by the way they view the world. Difference and diversity can be either celebrated or attacked, and it is important to be clear about the value base we use in order to assess what approach is appropriate. Abusive behaviours, for example, are certainly 'different and diverse', and characterize the way in which some people view the world. But the value base held by people professionals, that stresses the unique value of each person and their right to be respected and treated with dignity, challenges any worldview that suggests that anyone can be treated otherwise.

The attempt to operationalize these values can be seen sometimes as something of a 'rescue attempt' in that they will often seek at least to soften or ameliorate the impact of these negative forces and influences on the lives of the people they are working with. Women-centred practice, for example, often helps women to focus on the ways in which a patriarchal system has kept them in a secondary, subservient role. That realization, linked with some achievable strategic objectives, often helps women to take back control of their lives, and to be set free from the discriminatory and oppressive behaviour of others. It has also led to serious challenging of cultural and structural issues that have played a part in this sexist oppression.

For this reason, there has been an increasing focus upon emancipatory forms of practice, with their emphasis upon helping people to be 'set free from' some of the forces and influences that were having a negative impact upon their lives. Whether we tackle the processes that lead to oppression (anti-discriminatory practice), or deal with the oppression itself (anti-oppressive practice) the overall aim is emancipation from discriminatory and oppressive practices, assumptions, structures, language and so on.

The strength of this approach is that it takes seriously at personal, cultural and structural levels the very real negative forces that are at work within society and which diminish the life chances and opportunities of so many people. Until society can do something to change its shape, it will be important for people professionals to address such issues as best they can, within their admitted limitations. It is at this point, however, that the full richness of anti-discriminatory practice needs to be acknowledged: to be seen, in effect, not just as a strategy for tackling problems, serious though they are, but also as a pointer towards a true celebration of diversity.

'Celebrating diversity' has therefore become a sort of benchmark that seeks to establish a positive value statement to underpin best practice. This suggests that the best starting point is to celebrate the very real differences that people bring to a complex society, and to make a point of celebrating the diversity and the enrichment that this brings. This position will fight hard against discrimination and oppression, within a framework that clearly states that society will be the poorer if all parts of the community do not celebrate their full potential. Society will lack the colour and brightness, the vigour and talent that often lie untapped if there is not a positive statement about celebrating diversity at its very heart.

To move to such a position requires a commitment by the traditional majority groups to begin to see things differently. For too long the married, heterosexual white male, with a job, a mortgage and 2.4 children, two cars and a set of brown, green or black wheelie bins – oh yes, and of course a wife who may well wish to go out to work – has been seen as the societal norm. But times have changed, and society can now be infinitely enriched by different styles of family and lifestyle, ethnic and cultural traditions and various expressions of the work/leisure balance, not to mention the increasing diversity and richness of experience in the 'silver power' of older people in the community.

TIP! An important part of this is self-awareness which involves constantly asking yourself what assumptions you are making from your own perspective. How might other people with a different perspective see this situation? Our own perspective is just one of many.

The move towards celebrating diversity consciously recognizes and values the many types of contribution that can enrich a community and positively laments the negative impact upon the whole community when certain groups are prevented, for whatever reason, from making their contribution to the tapestry of its life together.

The significance of this for religion and spirituality is clear. The phrase 'emancipatory practice', for example, is one that is likely to ring bells within at least some faith communities. Both Christian and Jewish traditions, for example, share a common history of a people being 'set free' from tyrannical oppression and slavery. One aspect of their theological framework is of a divine Being who sets people free, and this is a theme that has had an enormous appeal to oppressed peoples who yearn for liberation and emancipation, as well as experiencing an inner freedom as individuals. There are close parallels between the PCS analysis discussed by Thompson and some of these theological insights that also challenge ways in which people can be discriminated against and oppressed at a structural level.

All of this, however, seems at times to be in marked contrast to the individualistic conceptualization and definition of spirituality and has probably served to alienate many people professionals who cannot see the links between spirituality and the struggle for social justice and emancipatory practice.

If, however, spirituality is understood in a much broader sense that allows – demands even – both cultural and structural dimensions to be included, then the picture changes radically:

> Within this framework, the loss of the spiritual is to be deeply mourned, and its gradual recovery something to be celebrated, precisely because of this deep-seated imperative to work at every level for the wholeness and

liberation of human beings from everything which enslaves and impoverishes the human spirit. In this sense there will be a powerful clash not between spirituality and those who are arguing passionately for, and striving ceaselessly for emancipatory practice, but rather *between these two new allies* on one side and on the other side the forces of organized religion which... have served at times to enslave and diminish and to control. Spirituality becomes... the very heart of the struggle for justice and emancipation.

(Moss, 2002, pp. 43–4)

That this remains a challenge for many helping professions is clear. With the notable exception of healthcare and medical professionals who at least have emphasized the contribution that religion and spirituality can play at an individual level, other people professions have largely avoided any acknowledgement of the contribution religion and spirituality can make to individual, let alone community wellbeing and enrichment. The vast resources of a variety of faith-based organizations being made available to the community for pastoral care, for example, have been regularly overlooked by social workers seeking to put together packages of care in the community.

This discussion has focused on the value base of anti-discriminatory practice within a framework of celebrating diversity. The close links between these frameworks and an understanding of spirituality that includes a passion for justice and emancipation have also been emphasized.

Exercise 29

Why, in your view, is celebrating diversity an important underpinning of spiritually sensitive practice? What might the negative consequences be if diversity is not valued?

CHAPTER 30

Challenging discrimination

Introduction

Considerable space has been devoted in this manual to an endeavour to present a balanced view about the positive and negative impact of religion and spirituality. Behind all these generalities, however, lies the truth that, for each person, the reality will be unique. How a person interprets and understands their spirituality will be unique to them and may never be fully articulated, however sensitively the dialogue with a professional may be conducted. Indeed, one of the difficulties with this whole area of these aspects of human experience is the unavoidable lack of clarity when defining the terms being used, linked to the fact that, for many people, the language of religion and spirituality seems foreign to their worldview. Spirituality is seen by them as a marginal 'activity' that excites the interest of the fanatical few, rather than something that illuminates and informs what it means for all of us to be human. And yet, from the perspective of the people professionals in whatever field or discipline, these are important issues to raise and grapple with, especially if it is accepted that resilience and a passion for justice are also part of this territory.

We are perhaps in a better position to explore the practice perspectives of our definition of spirituality as what we do to give expression to our chosen worldview now that the context of anti-discriminatory practice has been explored as the value base for the people professions. Furthermore, the suggestion that spirituality and/or religion can have a liberating, emancipatory role in people's lives that can foster resilience in dealing with the painful and sometimes tragic dimensions of human life is one that we need to take very seriously. Much of the work involves dealing with pain, change and loss in people's lives and to have a framework that can offer a creative context for understanding and dealing with these issues is of huge significance. At times of crisis, people tend to

DOI: 10.4324/9781003682318-34

ask the 'big' questions that raise issues about meaning and purpose in their lives and how to make sense of events that challenge their previously held worldview. The challenge of this manual is the extent to which they feel able to enter into some meaningful dialogue with people at this very point of inner discomfiture. In short, they can explore issues of spirituality, whether or not this word is actually used in their dialogue.

Our definition of spirituality allows us to explore with people how they see the world and what their chosen worldview looks like. Specifically, they can tease out the ways in which such worldviews enable the people who hold them to offer a (perhaps moderately) satisfying attempt to make sense of what is happening to them and to others, the extent to which their chosen worldview provides strength and resilience to deal with adversity and the framework it offers to them about how to regard and deal with other people. It is perhaps reasonable to suggest that, for a worldview to be credible, it must be able to a certain extent to satisfy all three of these criteria. In other words, for a worldview to be credible, it must be able to provide for the person who holds it:

1.   A satisfying framework to provide at least some answers to the 'big' questions about meaning and purpose in life;
2.   An emotionally satisfying impact that strengthens our capacity to deal with major losses and disasters, thereby increasing our resilience; and
3.   A value base for how we behave towards others.

The third criterion is of particular interest for people professionals who are often dealing with the impact of people's behaviour on others. Probation officers, prison officers, social workers, youth workers and managers in various settings, for example, will often be seeking to change people's problematic behaviour. To have any chance of successful change necessarily involves an exploration into the individual's worldview and to review the implications and limitations of the chosen worldview for that particular person. The work of prison chaplains is illuminating at this point. Some of the 'success stories' that are recounted by chaplains frequently involve a major change of worldview on the part of the particular prisoners whose determination to 'go straight' stems from a particular 'conversion experience'; in other words, they take on a different worldview that then profoundly affects how they choose to behave.

Professionals, of course, are not allowed to proselytize or to persuade people to adopt a different worldview. This fear has been at the heart of much disquiet within the education and training of helping professionals. The dangers of exploiting vulnerable people at times of emotional distress are well known. Interestingly, however, the concern has traditionally always been directed at helping professionals who espouse a particular religious affiliation. Christian workers, for example, are always challenged on this very issue to make sure that their religious commitment does not compromise their professional values, and that they do not seek to 'convert' people through their professional intervention. This is absolutely right and fully accepted. What is fascinating in this context is that people who hold an atheist position, for example, or people who are fundamentally opposed to any valuing of spirituality are not similarly challenged so explicitly. And yet, perhaps they need just as much professional training in how to work sensitively with people of faith as committed members of faith-based organizations need in avoiding the dangers of proselytizing. Both of these are examples of worldviews that may or may not meet the three criteria outlined above as far as each individual is concerned. The important issue for the people professions is the willingness, sensitivity and openness to explore these issues when appropriate with those who come to them for help.

Reflective moment

How would you feel if a professional who was helping you in some way sought to impose their worldview on you? What impact would this have on your feelings of trust towards that person?

One further example deserves mention, not least because it takes us into some complex issues for practice. Someone who belongs to a far-right organization, for example, may feel that their chosen worldview satisfies all three criteria. From the perspective of the professional worker, however, there would be major concerns about a value base/worldview that not only treats people of colour disrespectfully, but also actively encourages violence against them. This flies in the face of the 'celebrating diversity' value base of the professional worker so fundamentally that it has to be challenged. The discriminatory and oppressive behaviour that such a worldview encourages is so alien not just to the professional value base, but also to the law of the land that it has to be challenged. But the very act of challenging, with its demands that at the very least people modify their behaviour or pay the consequences has an element of proselytizing to it, in that respect for individual dignity should be a non-negotiable tenet.

The issue of racial discrimination is just one of many examples that could be chosen. Two further examples involve the way in which women are regarded and treated and how issues of human sexuality are dealt with, particularly within faith-based organizations. These are areas that often cause the greatest concern for people professionals when working in a multi-faith, multicultural community.

The issues can be stark precisely because some faith-based organizations adopt principled positions on these issues that are based on doctrinal convictions derived from interpretations from their sacred writings. To those who have had no involvement with faith communities, this can be a confusing territory to explore, not least because there is a rich variety of interpretation within most, if not all, faith traditions. Some traditions within the Christian Church, for example, are strongly committed to inclusivity as a basic tenet of faith. They believe that the creative God they worship loves people equally and unreservedly, and that diversity is a God-given gift to the world that needs to be reflected above all in the very communities that seek to give God their allegiance. Therefore, everybody, irrespective of race, gender, or sexual orientation, needs to feel that they have a part to play within the Church, including leadership at all levels. If such a stance seems to be at odds with tradition and the sacred texts, the response is that the same creative God is not restricted by the past but is ever leading people into newer and deeper understandings of what it means to be human.

By contrast, other traditions within the Christian Church claim to be just as loyal to their creator God and believe that they are under an obligation to respect, as they stand, the teachings of their sacred texts. If their interpretation of these texts means that women need to play a subservient role, and that only heterosexual love making within a legally binding marriage is acceptable, then they see it as their clear duty to proclaim this, even if it does mean being out of step with contemporary values. Of far greater importance to them is an obedience to what they believe are eternal and unchanging truths that have an impact on human behaviour. These examples may be followed through in the other main monotheistic religions (Judaism and Islam), although there seems to be less clear evidence within Islam of what some may call the 'liberal' approach to human sexuality. However, in Patel and colleagues' (1997) important book, one anonymous author comments powerfully, from an Asian female perspective, on the ways in which:

> Religious ethics are contaminated by a male political and economic agenda which turns women into dependants, and as a result, denies the equality, respect and control of their lives and the opportunity to contribute meaningfully to society.

(p. 54)

Key point

Religion, as we have seen, is a highly complex social phenomenon. We have to be very careful not to oversimplify by seeing religion in black and white terms when the reality is far more complicated, intricate and, in some ways, contradictory.

The perplexity felt by people professionals is understandable. In terms of the framework being proposed in this manual, it seems as if there is not just one Christian, Muslim or Jewish worldview, but several almost competing worldviews within each of these religions. And if the terms of reference are expanded to include the totality of religions, the confusion becomes absolute! And yet it is salutary to note that each of these faith-based organizations, whether they attract millions, thousands or only hundreds of adherents, are offering to their members a worldview that we must assume they find satisfying in terms of the three criteria offered earlier in this chapter. The challenge is not to feel that somehow they need to be 'expert' in their knowledge of these faith systems, but rather to feel confident and comfortable in exploring with people the ways in which their chosen worldview proves satisfying, and how it affects their behaviour especially towards others. So, the emphasis is less on 'knowing about' and much more on the worker's willingness, ability and sensitivity to explore these issues with people whose choice of worldview may be quite alien to their own. The role of the professional may be summarized as challenging discrimination and fostering resilience. The challenging of discrimination is, of course, familiar territory to many, especially social workers and probation officers. The value base discussed earlier provides a clear imperative for this. The particular sensitivity facing practitioners is when discrimination is practised in the name of a particular faith-based organization that otherwise would be deemed to be playing a positive and constructive role within society. In some communities, for example, the role of women appears to be understood in very clear ways and the expectations upon women to live within these boundaries is high. This can lead to some tensions between career and family expectations and a clash between competing worldviews, each of which genuinely believes that it is honouring and respecting the women in their community.

Here, of course, we enter the realms of very familiar debate about patriarchy, gender stereotyping, discrimination and oppression that are important searchlights to be played upon the whole of society, not just upon specific faith-based organizations. People professionals, however, often feel that the tightrope is more hazardous to balance on when dealing with faith-based organizations. Should they collude with a system they fundamentally disagree with or does a respectful, professional approach demand that we start where the other person is to be found, even if that feels compromising to the worker? These are practice dilemmas that have no easy answer. These dilemmas are perhaps at their most acute (or perhaps they are most straightforward?) when issues of abuse are being explored. Is male or female circumcision, for example, ever justifiable, even if entrenched in religious tradition? How do we respond to issues of family discipline that to the worker might seem too severe, but that the family believe are part of their religious responsibility? Professional judgement is crucial here, as is a system of detailed recording, supervision and accountability, but ultimately anti-discriminatory practice provides the framework to tackle these complex issues.

When it comes to fostering resilience, we enter the wide arena of assessment whereby we try to make sense of the situations we are involved with. The requirements to include a religious/spiritual dimension in our assessment of a situation have already been noted, even though this continues to be a much-neglected area. In all circumstances, resilience is an important factor to consider. As has already been argued, there is an important practice-focused link between a strengths perspective and resilience, both of which can be located within a spirituality framework.

It should not for one moment be assumed that a strengths perspective has a narrow focus for a professional. On the contrary, it is such a fundamental principle that it needs to be a core strand in the approach that all people professionals take. A strengths perspective starts from the assumption – or from the worldview – that everyone has strengths, gifts, talents and abilities that can be used in their life journey. There may well be occasions when major loss or trauma 'zaps' the energies and reduces a person's capacity to cope temporarily. But the role of the people professional is not to foster a sense of learnt helplessness or dependence, but rather to be an enabling encourager who seeks to bring back to full strength the talents and capacity that are present in that person. The current buzzwords of 'partnership working' and 'empowerment' are part of this process.

In the search for a particular person's strengths, it is important to take as holistic an approach as possible. It is here that the acknowledgement of spirituality and religion must be made. On some occasions, it may well be that the previously tried and trusted worldview has been blown apart or at least severely dented by the events that have brought the helping professional into their lives. In such cases, it may well fall upon the practitioner to begin a dialogue and a gentle exploration that ultimately a better qualified spiritual or religious leader may need to take further. But the importance of giving a message to the person that it is all right to discuss such issues cannot be underestimated. There are occasions when people who belong to faith communities, for example, find it difficult to talk to their religious or spiritual leaders about the loss of faith brought about by some major event because they feel they are 'letting the side down'. The core value of unconditional acceptance by the professional at this early stage may well play a major role in helping that person regain the strength they feel they have lost and to undertake the at times costly journey of reconstructing a worldview that helps them make more sense of what has happened to them.

For others, however, it is their spiritual perspective or their religious faith that sustains them through difficult days and casts a rainbow of meaning around their apparently dark and hostile sky. This can become clear at times of great loss or bereavement; or in a more general sense they have a conviction that their future 'is in safe hands'. The Muslim conviction, shared to a greater or lesser degree by other faith systems, that everything that happens must, by definition, be according to the will of Allah, may appear mystifying to a non-believer, but to a devout Muslim it brings a sense of confidence and peace. This only comes, of course, with the acceptance of the Islamic worldview, but it is an example of how resilience and a strengths perspective can be derived from a faith system. We need to acknowledge and respect such a view, even if it feels alien to our own worldview.

By contrast, a worker who belongs to a faith community would need to acknowledge and respect what we may call an 'atheistic spirituality', even if to them it seems to be a contradiction in terms. According to our definition of spirituality, however, such a position is perfectly tenable. Indeed, there are many who find strength and resilience precisely from the conviction that there is 'nothing more' to life or after life than what we can experience in our everyday living and loving. It is this sense of feeling more in control, rather than relying on some supreme being, that enhances their capacity for resilience. In such situations, best practice would be about acknowledging this and helping the person to celebrate their resilience, not about seeking to introduce a different worldview that the person had no wish, or need, to accept.

This chapter has explored two sides of a coin as far as practice issues are concerned. It has stressed the importance of a proper sense of discrimination that can distinguish between the good and bad effects of religion and spirituality, especially when it involves how people behave towards each other. It has re-emphasized the importance of the value base of anti-discriminatory practice as a benchmark by which to evaluate the criteria for an 'effective' worldview. It has further emphasized the ways in which a strengths perspective is an important approach for people professionals to take in all their work and that, for many people, spirituality in a general sense, and for some religions in particular, are important components for their own resilience that workers need to acknowledge and respect.

Exercise 30

In what ways might your own spiritual worldview potentially clash with the worldview of people you may be asked to work with in your professional capacity? How might you manage any such clashes effectively? What would you need to take into account?

CHAPTER 31

Religion, spirituality and mental health

Introduction

There is always a risk in a chapter such as this that those who feel an affinity with the topic area will press on and read it, while others that the subject holds less interest for will simply skip over and ignore it. It is for this reason that the main thrust and approach of the manual has been to deal with issues in a general way, rather than trying to unpack a series of perhaps 'single issue' topics. Mental health has been chosen, however, for several reasons, principally the following two. First, it is one of the comprehensive topics that cannot be limited to particular age groups people professionals work with and is increasingly being recognized as an important set of workplace issues for managers. It is a pervasive and complex phenomenon that can affect us all. Second, it has attracted considerable interest among practitioners and academics who are fascinated by the interfaces across religion, spirituality and mental health in our multi-faith, multicultural society.

There is now an increasing recognition of the importance of 'recovery' as a challenge to the longstanding – but mistaken – assumption that people with mental health problems cannot move beyond them. It is a significant development in contributing to a 'whole person' approach that identifies and develops a person's resilience as part of that process. It will be precisely through the spending of 'quality time' with people – if that is not too hackneyed a phrase – that the prospects of recovery will be enhanced. And in that process, the chances are high that each individual's chosen worldview will be uncovered and the theme of spirituality, especially when linked to the concepts of a strengths perspective and resilience, will be encountered as part of their journey to recovery.

For too long a 'popular view' has prevailed that associates religion and spirituality with psychiatric and psychological problems: hallucinations; hearing

DOI: 10.4324/9781003682318-35

voices; seeing visions; and generally manifesting a 'quirky' worldview that needed 'treatment' so that 'normality' could return.

It may be helpful at this point to offer a brief review of some of the evidence about the positive impact of religion and spirituality upon mental health. We may perhaps take as read some of the more negative reactions people have experienced, such as a burdensome, disabling sense of guilt and sin and lack of self-worth exacerbated by certain religious traditions; suicidal thoughts and actions sometimes on a community level (for example, the mass suicide at Waco, Texas, instigated by a self-styled religious leader); and the 'brainwashing' especially of young people by certain religious sects and communities.

By contrast, it has now been established for quite some time that spirituality and religion can play a key part in a person's psychological wellbeing; or as Powell (2003, p. 1) aptly puts it: 'spirituality is good for your health'. He further observes that some research findings show that:

> The majority of people coping with mental disorder find themselves turning to their spiritual and religious beliefs to help them pull through. For instance, in one survey of psychiatric patients, over half went to religious services and prayed daily, and over 80 per cent felt that their spiritual beliefs had a positive impact on their illness, providing comfort and feeling of being cared for and not alone.
>
> (p. 1)

Religion and spirituality can no longer be disregarded: on the contrary, they do seem to play a prominent role in recovery and well-being, and people professionals need to recognize this important dimension (Mochon et al., 2011).

There does seem to be a close parallel between the training issues in spirituality for mental health professionals and for other people professionals. It is not only social workers whose curricula often do not take these issues seriously; probation officers, youth workers, advice workers and managers are likely to face a similar lack of serious exploration of these issues on their training courses.

In addition, whatever hesitations some may have about the suggestion of an extremely high predisposition towards spirituality and religion on the part of people who have mental health difficulties, it should be clear that spirituality and religion need to be at least placed on the map and taken seriously. If we are able to affirm the positive contribution religion and spirituality can make towards positive mental health generally, and to increasing the resilience and strength perspectives for people recovering from mental health problems, then again, the issues need to be placed firmly on the training and education agenda.

Furthermore, people who experience mental health difficulties often find their worldview is challenged. People, and frames of reference, that previously had seemed reliable can begin to appear to be less trustworthy. While it is perfectly true that a return to robust health can be accompanied by a return of confidence in the previous worldview, for others the experience of mental health problems can lead to a reshaping of a worldview that remains intact after recovery has been achieved. The emphasis being made in this manual upon the importance of a worldview, and what we do to give expression to it, therefore becomes particularly significant in issues to do with mental health.

Key point

Mental health problems have traditionally been seen in individualistic terms as forms of illness, but this narrow medical view is increasingly being challenged by more holistic perspectives that argue for the need to also incorporate social and spiritual aspects as key factors in shaping people's mental wellbeing (see, for example, Thompson, 2019b).

Finally, it is important to recognize that, no matter in what area of practice we work, many people will feel unable to raise anything to do with religion and spirituality, even though these may be significant features in their own journey to recovery. They are likely to feel that this is a 'no go' area as far as therapeutic support is concerned. This raises important issues for anyone working in the people professions, including managers who are increasingly being expected to address workplace mental health issues. To what extent do we consciously or subconsciously give off messages to those we work with that there are certain 'no go' areas we do not wish them to trespass into? That we all have such areas is beyond doubt, and for many the territory of religion and spirituality is one any journeying into, however tentative, seems to be fraught with uncertainty, even anxiety. This is the key point: it is the professional's worldview that is somehow being challenged and until we can reach the point where we can show the respect and dignity to those who wish, and at times really need, to talk about such issues with us, then we shall never reach that ultimate goal of 'best practice' that all of the people we support so deeply deserve. The implication of this, however, is that there is an obligation upon all people professionals to have a sufficiently mature level of self-awareness to be comfortable enough with these issues to share that journey with those they are seeking to help and not to allow any misgivings or their own particular and different worldview to put up the 'no entry' barriers for people who face such issues as an important feature of their landscape.

Exercise 31

In what ways do you feel mental health problems can be linked to spiritual needs and challenges? How might a focus on spirituality contribute positively to mental health care?

CHAPTER 32

Values-based practice

Introduction

In an earlier work (Thompson and Moss, 2026), we emphasized the central role of values as a key underpinning of practice. We argued that:

> Many people make the mistake of assuming that values are abstract things unconnected with the reality of their day-to-day lives. Nothing could be further from the truth. Everything we do is touched by our values, by those principles and beliefs that we hold dear.

> (p. tbc)

Some people are very aware of what their values are and can make them explicit, but for many others, values are things they have rarely, if ever, given any thought to. However, that does not alter the fact that values are a major influence on our thoughts, feelings and actions – they influence us regardless of whether we are aware of them or give them any consideration.

The point we want to emphasize here is that values are part of our spirituality. They are significant in terms of our sense of who we are and how we fit into the world; they play a part in making our lives meaningful and giving us a sense of purpose and direction. And, of course, they relate closely to connectedness, to how we connect with other people and with matter greater than ourselves. If we want to develop a genuinely spiritually sensitive practice, then we need to make sure that we are paying attention to the important role of values.

Anti-discriminatory practice

In discussing values, we have emphasized the importance of equality, diversity and inclusion in the form of anti-discriminatory practice. This is partly because

DOI: 10.4324/9781003682318-36

our practice is unlikely to be effective if we are allowing discrimination and oppression to continue unchecked (or, worse still, actually contributing to such discrimination and oppression) – we cannot expect to build trust and form viable partnerships in such circumstances. It is also partly because it would be unethical to fail to address racism, sexism or whatever other form of discrimination we should come across – we cannot truly call ourselves professionals if we are behaving in ways that are fundamentally unethical. It is essential, therefore, that we are 'tuned in', as it were to discrimination issues and do not allow ourselves to become complacent.

Other important values

Important though these issues are, we also need to make sure that we are aware of – and committed to – other important value considerations, such as the following:

- *Respect and dignity* These are, of course, important 'lubricants' of social interaction, but they are also part of what makes us decent human beings. This is self-evident, but what is not so obvious is that busy, tired, stressed, anxious, frustrated or (semi-)burnt out people professionals are no more immune to losing sight of respect and dignity than anyone else.
- *Confidentiality* Confidential information is sensitive material that we are being trusted with. If we fail to live up to that trust, we can do a lot of harm. This is especially the case for people who find it difficult to trust (as a result of being abused or traumatized in another way, for example), as we could end up adding to their problems, rather than contributing to addressing them.
- *Empowerment* Helping people gain greater control over their lives is what empowerment is all about. This helps to build trust and enables people to feel more comfortable with who they are (an important spiritual consideration). Our own urge to be helpful and valued (another spiritual consideration) can at times lead us into taking over and putting ourselves in the driving seat rather than help the person(s) we are supporting to take charge of their own lives.

This is just a selection of the important values that we need to be aware of. We hope that this sample will be enough to highlight the links between values and spirituality.

Key point

Values influence us whether or not we are aware of them. But, for the best results in terms of professional practice, it pays to be as fully aware as we can of what our values are (both personal and professional) to ensure that we are acting with integrity – that is, consistently with those values.

Other people's values

In the people professions, it is not only our own values that are significant. We have emphasized the importance of strengths and resilience, and people's values can be of major significance in this regard. People can gain great strength from 're-connecting' with their values. For example, managers can help disengaged employees to reinvest in their work by revisiting the values that brought them into that type of work in the first place.

TIP! To make sure that you do not lose sight of your values, it can be very helpful to make them explicit – that is, to make a list of what they are, why they are important to you and how they affect your work and your life more broadly.

The role of reassurance

From our extensive work in relation to loss and grief we have become very aware of the crucial role of solace and reassurance. As we noted earlier, when someone is grieving (or dying), we cannot take the pain away, but through human warmth and concern, we can make the bearing of it easier and less lonely and frightening.

However, we would want to add that the powerful role of reassurance is one that is often underappreciated in a variety of contexts, not just in relation to death, grief or bereavement. As Kneale (2013) puts it:

> If heaven and morality are not the key elements of all religions, then what is? The answer, I would suggest, is *reassurance*. From the earliest times every religion has given people comfort by offering ways – so their followers believe – of keeping their worst nightmares at bay.
>
> (p. 7)

As in all matters spiritual, religion is a major player, but not the only one. Valuable reassurance can come from a wide range of sources, not least from the skilled work of people professionals.

Exercise 32

What do you think the adverse consequences of losing sight of our values could be in (i) our professional capacity; and (ii) our personal lives? How can we make sure that we stay connected with our values?

CHAPTER 33

Obstacles to spiritual fulfilment

Introduction

Spiritual fulfilment can be understood as a state of deep contentment and connection with something larger than oneself. It is often seen as a basic existential challenge, its achievement being something that we strive for, perhaps reaching it at times, but not at others. We discussed earlier the idea of life as a journey involving a spiritual path and spiritual support often taking the form of others being fellow travellers on that path. That path is rarely straightforward and we will meet many challenges along the way, as well as many joys that generally make the journey a worthwhile one.

Spiritual fulfilment is sadly not guaranteed. As we shall see, there are many potential obstacles. This chapter examines some of the major ones, but by no means covers all the possibilities. However, what we do cover should alert you to the issues that need to be considered and give you the opportunity to consider how to rise to the challenges involved.

Materialism

Capitalism is based on the generation of profits, and so for capitalist economies to succeed, sales need to keep happening. As a result of this, there is a great emphasis – in the media, for example – on the sale of material goods. An ideology has developed that presents the purchase of material goods as an important basis of not only happiness, but also status and prestige (conspicuous consumption, as it is often called). Despite the dominance of this 'consumerist' thinking, there is a growing emphasis on the longstanding recognition of the

DOI: 10.4324/9781003682318-37

need to move away from such a reliance (Schumacher, 1973). As Harari (2015) wisely puts it:

> When Epicurus defined happiness as the supreme good, he warned his disciples that it is hard work to be happy. Material achievements alone will not satisfy us for long. Indeed, the blind pursuit of money, fame and pleasure will only make us miserable. Epicurus recommended, for example, to eat and drink in moderation, and to curb one's sexual appetites. In the long run, a deep friendship will make us more content than a frenzied orgy.
>
> (pp. 18–19)

It may not be strictly true that the love of money is the root of all evil, but it is certainly the case that materialism brings a number of problems that can stand in the way of spiritual fulfilment. However, the myth that wealth necessarily brings happiness continues to drive a high proportion of people in the direction of consumerism. As Loy (2010) has argued: 'Consumerism is not merely about acquiring things; it's a way of life that structures our desires and shapes our sense of self' (p. 112). This leads us in nicely to the next obstacle.

Reflective moment

To what extent do material considerations influence your life and your happiness? Are there ways in which you can bring a more spiritual dimension to your life?

The tyranny of the ego

Closely related to the problem of materialism is what has come to be known as the tyranny of the ego (Tolle, 2005). This refers to the tendency to focus narrowly on ourselves and be primarily concerned with our own self-centred needs and concerns and, in doing so, losing sight of the bigger picture and the benefits of empathy and compassion. A key part of this is competitiveness, a constant striving to do better than others, to show some sort of superiority. While competitiveness in itself is not necessarily a bad thing, when it comes to predominating, it can stand in the way of positive nurturing and empowering relationships with others. People come to be seen first and foremost as rivals, rather than potential fellow participants in mutually beneficial arrangements.

A person suffering from the tyranny of the ego is likely to have a preoccupation with the superficial aspects of life and thus be distracted from an inner spiritual journey, hindering the development of genuine self-awareness and compassion and the enrichment they bring. It can prevent us from engaging with such important issues as meaning, purpose and direction, leaving us feeling quite empty and unfulfilled, with no real sense of connectedness.

Stress and burnout

The 'buzz' of modern life can be stimulating, motivating and rewarding, but when pressures are too great or go on for too long without respite, the result can be harmful, health-affecting stress (Thompson, 2024b). Rapid and multiple changes in the world of work (Cheese, 2021) have placed immense pressures on a significant proportion of people, making stress one of the most common reasons for absence from work and, indeed, for staff turnover (Saks and Gruman, 2021).

It is, of course, difficult if not impossible to feel spiritually fulfilled if you feel that you are drowning under the weight of pressures you are facing, whether these derive from the workplace, your home life or a mixture of the two. Tackling stress is therefore not only a health and safety issue, but also a spiritual challenge. Enlightened employers would therefore do well to bear in mind that a commitment to workplace wellness has a spiritual dimension (Thompson, 2025a).

Closely related to stress is the problem of burnout. Characterized by feelings of energy depletion or exhaustion, a sense of detachment or disengagement and a negative or cynical attitude and a lower level of effectiveness, productivity, it can be understood as an attempted solution to the problem of stress. That is, by emotionally and spiritually withdrawing from their over-pressurized circumstances, people so affected are trying to find a way of coping with the overload. Unfortunately, though, it is generally an ineffective strategy and is likely to create a vicious circle in which it makes coping with the pressures more, rather than less, difficult.

Clearly, once again we are in the realm of spirituality.

Key point

It is quite common for people who are stressed and/or burnt out to clearly show that this is the case (through their body language, for example. However, it is important to be aware that not everybody makes their distress visible, or at least not obvious – they have learnt out how to mask it. It is therefore important to be aware that signs of stress and burnout can be quite subtle or even totally absent. Openness about such issues is therefore essential.

Unresolved grief and trauma

Grief is commonly regarded as an emotional reaction to a significant loss, but in reality it is a four-dimensional reaction (Thompson, 2022): not only emotional, but also physical or biological, social and – significantly – spiritual. People who are grieving can temporarily lose their sense of purpose and direction and experience what is known as 'biographical disruption' that is, they can feel that they no longer know who they are, such has been the level and intensity of disruption to their life. As we discussed in Chapter 25, grieving can be understood as a process of rebuilding frameworks of meaning that have been destabilized or even destroyed by the loss and characterized by a to-ing and fro-ing between intense feelings of loss and steps to build a new reality in the absence of who or what has been lost. There is clearly a spiritual dimension to this.

Grief is a process of adjusting to the major disruptions brought about one or more losses. Although it tends to be painful, exhausting and frightening, it is basically a positive process of healing. However, in some circumstances, the process is prolonged or 'gets stuck' and the grief remains unresolved. The spiritual challenges involved can therefore continue over a significant period of time and thereby serve as a major obstacle to spiritual fulfilment. As people professionals (including managers) we should therefore be tuned in to situations when people may need additional help in addressing the grief challenges they face.

Psychosocial trauma can also be seen as significant in this regard. In a very real sense, trauma can be seen as a severe form of grief and can affect people in the same way. Traumatic experiences if not resolved can create a number of problems and once again, a barrier to spiritual fulfilment can be one of them. Unresolved trauma can prevent people from relaxing, feeling secure (see the discussion of ontological security earlier) or functioning at an optimal level. It can be an obstacle to trusting people and thereby serve as a blockage when it comes to developing positive relationships, whether in work or outside it. This can prevent a positive sense of connectedness from developing, and confusion over the future can stand in the way of a helpful sense of meaning, purpose and direction.

Information overload

The technology that has become fairly standard and mainstream in the digital age presents another significant obstacle to spiritual fulfilment. The development of social media with its relentless flood of information and interruptions, combined with the ease of access to wider worlds of information through the internet and satellite television, has created major dangers of information overload. The emergence of artificial intelligence as a further major source of information is clearly compounding the problem. Our senses can be overwhelmed and our attention fragmented, making it difficult to cultivate any sense of inner stillness and focus. See Hari, 2022, for an interesting but disturbing account of the problems associated with an 'always on' society. Haidt (2024) raises similar concerns in relation to the impact on children.

Harari (2015) captures the situation well when he points out that:

> Today our knowledge is increasing at breakneck speed, and theoretically we should understand the world better and better. But the very opposite is happening. Our new-found knowledge leads to faster economic social and political changes; in an attempt to understand what is happening, we

accelerate the accumulation of knowledge, which leads only to faster and greater upheavals. Consequently, we are less and less able to make sense of the present or forecast the future.

(p. 67)

This constant stimulation can create a sense of restlessness and anxiety and thereby block spiritual growth and prevent spiritual fulfilment.

Anxiety and depression

We address anxiety and depression together because we see them as, in a sense, two sides of the same coin. We see the linking thread as the management of tension. Anxiety is a natural (and helpful) response to danger. However, it becomes a problem when we overreact (the reaction is disproportionate to the danger faced), react when it is not necessary (what we perceive as a danger is not actually a threat) or reach the point where anxiety is our normal, standard response to situations in general. In a sense, anxiety problems involve an amplification of tension.

With depression, what happens can be understood as a way of dealing with tension by withdrawing into ourselves, developing a sort of protective shell that dampens down the tension or blocks it out. It is as if painful and worrying circumstances have led to a sort of emotional (and spiritual) numbness that keeps the level of tension manageable, albeit at a cost.

The linking thread of tension partly explains why so many people experience problems with both anxiety and depression, as if they are struggling to find the healthy balance between the two, with tensions being managed effectively. Needless to say, both these problem circumstances, whether individually or together, can serve as a significant obstacle to spiritual fulfilment.

What is more, both of these can lead to very destructive vicious circles, with either anxiety spiralling out of control or depression becoming deeper and deeper, in each case becoming quite disabling.

Lack of community and connection

Hari (2018), in a thought-provoking study of the importance of 'connections' highlights the problems that can arise when modern industrialized societies prove to be inimical to a sense of community, connectedness and belonging. A key term here is 'social capital', as discussed earlier. The more connections we have with supportive individuals, groups and organizations, the stronger a position we are in to face life's challenges and the more resilient we are likely to be – and, of course, the more likely it will be that we will be able to find spiritual fulfilment.

This partly relates to the materialism discussed earlier in this chapter, with its tendency to focus more on material goods than on social and community connections. Linked to this is the tendency of the caring professions to be largely focused on the individual level. For example, at one time, groupwork and community work were staple parts of social work and drew on the power of bringing people together in constructive shared endeavours. Today, both groupwork and community work tend to be largely marginalized in both social work education and practice, another reflection of the influence of neoliberalism.

Discrimination and oppression

Given our comments so far on the detrimental effects of discrimination and oppression, it should come as no surprise to learn that we see these phenomena as significant barriers to spiritual fulfilment and spiritual growth. However, we would want to emphasize two points. First, we should note that many people have found spiritual sustenance by succeeding in challenging discrimination and oppression and/or managing to flourish despite them (for example, feminist groups who have made great progress in tackling patriarchy and have benefited from the solidarity engendered).

Second, we should also include poverty as part of this scenario. People wrestling with poverty and deprivation will often be discriminated against in a number of ways, not least simply because they are poor. It does not take too much imagination to work out that such circumstances can make spiritual fulfilment difficult (but not impossible) to achieve.

> **TIP!** Discrimination and oppression affect people in different ways and to different extents depending on a number of factors. Be careful not to jump to conclusions about the spiritual consequences of discrimination and oppression. As always, these are complex and sensitive issues.

Essentialism

We have already encountered this concept of essentialism, the belief that people have a fixed personality with very limited capacity for change. This myth, albeit quite widespread, can act as a brake on spiritual growth. If people believe that change and growth are not possible, then that becomes a self-fulfilling prophecy – it serves as a self-defeating belief. As such, this needs to be added to our list of obstacles to spiritual fulfilment.

Helping people break free from the restrictions of essentialism can be a very empowering way forward. This is not always easy, but there are various tools that can be used to make progress in this regard (Thompson, 2025c).

Cynicism

The term 'cynic' comes from the Greek word for dog, In simple terms, a cynic avoids making an emotional investment in success, politics or ideals, as they see them as pointless. Instead of committing to something positive, they often criticize what others believe in. It is sure route to negativity and defeatism and, as such, quite a problem when it comes to spiritual fulfilment or growth.

Adopting a cynical attitude tinges everything with negativity and is therefore self-defeating. As Eckhart Tolle (1999) puts it: 'The primary cause of unhappiness is never the situation but your thoughts about it' (p. 12). It is as if everything is seen through a negative filter.

One important point to note is that cynicism should not be confused with scepticism. Being sceptical means adopting a healthy questioning approach, rather than just accepting things at face value. This is very different from cynicism which involves adopting a *rejecting* attitude, rather than a questioning one.

Conclusion

There are no simple formula solutions to these challenging problems but, by being aware of them, we are much better placed when it comes to addressing them, preventing them in the first place or supporting people through the frustrations and turbulences involved.

Exercise 33

In your (intended) field of work, which three of these are likely to feature most and what could you possibly do to address the difficulties involved?

Epilogue

This manual does not have a definitive conclusion or a neat and tidy ending. With such issues as the ones we have been grappling with, a conclusion might suggest that the journey has reached a far more clearly defined destination than it has. Instead, an epilogue is offered, not just because it has a slightly religious or spiritual ring to it, but because it suggests the appropriateness of some closing comments as we pause to take breath on the next stage of the journey.

Some huge themes have been attempted in exploring and trying to bring some definition to what are admittedly complex and contentious issues. One principal aim however has been to argue that religion and spirituality are not the marginal activities and worldviews that many would claim them to be, and which cause some people professionals to consign them to their trash can of irrelevance. On the contrary, there are many influences now at work that mean that these issues need to be given the serious attention they deserve.

This has inevitably meant that the perplexing question of definition has had to be tackled. The literature has already offered a range of interesting and helpful definitions that have been reviewed in this manual, and which many have found to be helpful and illuminating. In offering our definition – that spirituality is what we do to give expression to our chosen worldview – it has not been our intention to add to the confusion but rather to offer an approach that can be helpful in tackling the range of issues that come their way. This 'practice-orientated' definition gives to practitioners and managers a 'handle' to develop ways of tackling these complex themes, without giving the impression that the people we support (or even we ourselves) have to learn a completely new language before we can begin

DOI: 10.4324/9781003682318-38

to communicate in this area. It offers a genuinely interested approach to someone by enquiring into:

- what 'turns that person on' and makes their life worthwhile;
- what gives them a sense of meaning and purpose;
- why do they do 'this set of things' rather than 'that set of things' and behave in this way rather than that way;
- what sustains them in times of crisis and difficulty; and
- how far is an experience of resilience being developed through their chosen worldview.

All these topics have been seen in the preceding discussions to be in the territory of spirituality – whether religious or otherwise – to a greater or lesser degree. In this sense at least, people may find themselves using slightly different language to describe already familiar experiences and approaches to life. The 'penny may suddenly drop' for some, as they encounter the definition being offered here: 'So, that is what is meant! I hadn't realized before!'.

This definition also seeks to overcome what is so often seen as the religion-spirituality 'divide'. Often the discussions tend to present religion as a bad thing and spirituality as a good thing. Tempting though this may be to some, it is a false divide. For one thing, it ignores the potential for positive and negative influences to be at work in both phenomena. To suggest that one can be all good and the other all bad is naive in the extreme. Our definition seeks, by contrast, to provide for the professional a template that can be used to evaluate the impact and influence that a person's worldview has upon their attitudes, values and behaviour. To what extent does a person's chosen worldview enrich their understanding of the world and the people they live and work with? How far does it spur them on to promote social justice, or to what extent does it make them adopt discriminatory behaviour towards others? To what extent does their worldview encourage them to celebrate diversity or to become narrowly partisan and bigoted? In other words, this definition enables the professional to explore the impact of a person's religion and spirituality in very practical and applied ways.

It has further implications for the professional. This definition moves beyond the approach that is often taken by educators and trainers who see the issue being best tackled by giving as much information as possible about various faith-based communities, their customs, beliefs and practices, so that professionals, in whatever sphere they choose to practise, will be well informed. Without doubt, in our multicultural, multi-faith society, all people professionals need to have developed a degree of multicultural, multi-faith awareness in order to offer a sensitive service to any who come to them. But, any hope of becoming fully informed is a myth: the more we learn about religion and spirituality, the more we realize how much more there is to learn. By contrast, our approach encourages the professional to explore with the people they support what are the implications in their lives of their chosen worldview, whether or not it has a specifically faith-based dimension.

This definition also makes it clear that the service provider/service recipient or manager/subordinate divide is by no means as clear cut as many think. Of course, there are professional boundaries that must be observed and best practice demands that an appropriate, well-thought through and partnership-based approach to the issues being raised is developed and implemented. But eventually the professional will walk away, and the person being supported will be left, it is to be hoped, better able to face the future more creatively than before but no longer needing professional support. All this is important and is rightly stressed. But, unlike some areas of contact where the professional may well feel that they have nothing in common with the person they are working with and that they are as different as 'chalk and cheese', when it comes to the definition offered in this manual, there is a commonality between them that some might find disconcerting. It is not just the people we support who choose a worldview: everyone does, implicitly or explicitly. All involved have a chosen worldview that has an impact upon their values, their behaviour and the way in which they treat other people. Everyone has gone through a similar process of deciding what the world is like and how we are to respond to it, even if the responses we come up with radically differ. From the practice perspective, this definition allows everyone to recognize that this is common territory in being human. The professional must not, of course, seek to 'convert' a service user to the worker's own chosen worldview, whether that be faith based or not, but the common shared experience of living as a consequence of a chosen worldview is something that can enrich a practitioner's work.

The definition, however, is not self-standing from a practice perspective. It has been stated clearly that there is a professional value base that underpins it and which in some ways provides an interpretative template to help a practitioner engage with the person coming to them for help and to evaluate their behaviour. The core value base of anti-discriminatory practice, incorporating a strengths perspective and a development of resilience in the face of adversity, is an impressive and fundamental foundation upon which all practice should be built. Important though spirituality and religion are in many people's lives, and even if in some respects their adherents may sometimes make claims that are 'beyond this world', when it comes to practice, the value base of anti-discriminatory practice in all its richness must remain intact.

Afterword

As explained in the Preface, this manual is a collaboration between two friends and colleagues who shared a strong interest in religion and spirituality but who approached the subject matter from very different angles – one the leader of a faith community and the other an atheistic existentialist. However, despite our different starting points, we were fully in agreement on a number of major points:

1. Spirituality is vitally important to everyone, not just to people who subscribe to a particular religion. Everyone has spiritual needs and faces spiritual challenges.
2. Religion is a major source of spirituality, but it is not the only one. The tendency to assume that faith communities have a monopoly on spirituality fails to recognize the major sources of spirituality that lie outside religion.
3. Where people do have a religious faith, it is essential for people professionals to be respectful of this and accordingly take into account the worldview of the individual(s) concerned. For very many people, religion is a significant part of their life and who they are. Ignoring this presents a distorted and potentially discriminatory picture.
4. Religion can do a lot of good, but also a lot of harm. Having a simplistic view of religion and its role in contemporary society is both misleading and potentially highly problematic. Much depends on not only the nature of the religion itself but also how that religion is manifested in practice. As with any philosophy or set of beliefs, it is not uncommon for there to be a discrepancy between what is expected to happen and what actually does.

5. Regardless of our own views about religion, as people professionals our role is neither to promote it, nor attack it. We are, of course, entitled to our own personal views and beliefs, but trying to deny other people their views and beliefs is not ethically sound.

I hope that what we have offered throughout the manual has helped you to understand what we mean by these points and why they are important. We regard them as the foundations of what we have been calling spiritually sensitive practice.

It is a great pity that Bernard did not survive to see this work published. However, I am delighted that we had already done enough planning prior to his death to enable me to build on those foundations and complete the project. The fact that, despite our differing 'angles' on religion, we were fully in agreement about the central role of spirituality and the need, as professionals, to respect other people's belief systems also made completing the manual a lot more straightforward.

From start to finish since our working relationship began many years ago, it has been an honour, privilege and pleasure to work with such an intelligent, well-educated, distinguished, insightful, caring and compassionate scholar of great integrity. In bringing this manual to a close I pay tribute to Bernard, as it stands as testimony to his major contribution to education and training in this area.

Dr Neil Thompson

Guide to further learning

This manual can only be seen as an introduction to the key themes that have been explored. It will have served its purpose well if it quickens the interest in those who read it and encourages them on a journey to discover more about these key issues.

However, the spirit this manual has been written in suggests that the starting point for further learning is not to hare round to the library, or into a Google search for key terms in order to increase the volume of information at our command. We have already noted that this would be a task of gigantic proportions, doomed to ultimate disappointment. Instead, it is suggested that the best place to start is with ourselves, and our own personal journey.

In Ancient Greece, much store was laid upon the oracle at Delphi where pilgrims would go to receive insight and wisdom. They were greeted with the inscription 'know thyself', and this perhaps is the best place for any of us to begin. Spirituality has been defined in this manual in terms that many, perhaps all, people professionals can identify with. We all have a chosen worldview, and how we live our lives, in large ways or small, is in response to that. So, a major starting point is this personal reflection about who we are, and what are the priorities we place centre stage in our own lives.

The big questions that were identified earlier in this manual are big questions for us too.

- How do we cope in the face of adversity?
- Are we resilient? In what ways does our worldview enhance that resilience? Or, if we are honest, do we find our worldview is a bit ragged round the edges at times and does not really 'pass muster'?

- What 'colours of meaning' do we throw round our lives to make some sense at least of what happens to us and those around us?
- What meaning do we give to our mortality?
- What does it mean to be human and to have the capacity to change?

How each of us deals with these and other equally profound questions is very much a matter of personal choice, of course. Some will find the framework of a faith community's worldview satisfying; others will look elsewhere. But it is important that somehow each of us develops that level of self-awareness, so that we feel comfortable about the journey it entails. For these are the journeys many of the people we serve are also making, however vaguely the details may be articulated. And, if we cannot share that journey to some extent at least, we are not providing a best-practice framework for our professional encounters with them.

It would be unwise to underestimate the importance of human contact in this journey. There is in some ways no substitute for meeting with people who hold particular worldviews to explore with them their significance and the impact their views have upon their behaviour. Whether or not you belong to a faith community, it can be helpful to arrange to meet and discuss issues with people who see the world from a different perspective. Study sessions or seminars can be held with invited guests to explore together some issues of common concern, for it is in the experience of the shared journey that the most effective learning can take place. It is also in the experience of a shared vulnerability – who among us has all the answers! – that a deeper enrichment can be shared. The shared concern to discover what various people do 'to give expression to their chosen worldview' is in itself an aspect of spirituality we all can participate in, particularly if we have a commitment to reflective practice. Such issues can even make their way onto supervision agendas at individual and team level.

Within this spirit of honest enquiry, however, where we recognize that the journey can at times be as much ours as of those who we seek to help, there is an increasing range of material to help and encourage us on this journey.

Each of the books mentioned here can offer some useful insights into the themes explored in this manual, and the reading lists that each of these contains can send people on a further journey of discovery.

There is an increasing number of useful websites available. These include:

www.thegoodwebguide.co.uk – useful as a navigation tool around world religions

www.beliefnet.com – this provides a one-step gateway to gain the views of various religions on current issues, as well as providing information about core beliefs (NB: You need to register on this site, but registration is free). http://about.com/religion has chapters on various issues of topical interest. There are websites produced by particular churches that also have a wider appeal and interest. The Church of England, for example, offers two: www.anglicansonline.org and www.anglicancommunion.org.

Similarly, the Roman Catholic Church offers a variety of sites. The following is worth looking at because of its emphasis upon social justice issues, and against extremism: www.cafod.org.uk – obviously focusing on the work of CAFOD (the Catholic Agency for Overseas Development); this site illustrates very vividly 'faith in action' and the social justice aspect of spirituality.

Two sites from a Jewish perspective are http://aish.com and www.chiefrabbi. org. The latter being particularly interesting to see how a religious leader tackles issues of extremism.

Islam

https://islamqa.com/en – this provides a range of Muslim perspectives, while www.islamicity.com takes a clear stand against extremism.

Hinduism

www.hindu.org – covers a wide range of issues and approaches to various religious perspectives in a non-judgemental and very informative way.

Paganism

www.druidnetwork.org - provides fascinating insights into the growing appeal of this fast-growing faith-based community.

In the fast-moving world of internet information, it is always best to explore issues of interest through a major search engine and discover just how much there is out there on these fascinating themes. It is worth noting, however, that it is not always easy to judge the 'bona fides' of websites that claim to represent various religious and/or spiritual perspectives. Here, as elsewhere on the internet, a degree of caution is necessary in order to distinguish between official sites that seek to reflect the beliefs and activities of a particular faith-based organization and other less official and more individualistic sites that seek to push a particular point of view.

Books

There is a huge literature around religion and associated forms of spirituality and a growing literature around non-religious approaches to spirituality. The following suggestions are therefore just the tip of the iceberg.

Armstrong, K. (1999) *A History of God: From Abraham to the Present: The 4000-year Quest for God*, London, Vintage.
Armstrong, K. (2006) *The Great Transformation: The World in the Time of Buddha, Socrates, Confucius and Jeremiah*, London, Atlantic Books.
Armstrong, K. (2010) *The Case for God: What Religion Really Means*, London, Vintage.

Bae, J. (2024) *The Book of Juju: Africana Spirituality for Healing, Liberation, and Self-Discovery*, Carlsbad, CA, Hay House.

Canda, E. R., Furman, L. D. and Canda, H-J. (2020) *Spiritual Diversity in Social Work Practice: The Heart of Helping*, 3rd edn, Oxford, Oxford University Press.

Clarke, P. B. (ed.) (2011) *The Oxford Handbook of the Sociology of Religion*, Oxford, Oxford University Press.

The Dalai Lama (2013) *Beyond Religion: Ethics for a Whole World*, London, Rider.

Doss, E. (2023) *Spiritual Moderns: Twentieth-Century American Artists and Religion*, Chicago, IL, University of Chicago Press.

Flanagan, K. and Jupp, P. C. (eds) (2010) *A Sociology of Spirituality*, Farnham, Ashgate.

Garcia, D. (2022) *The God Who Riots: Taking Back the Radical Jesus*, Minneapolis, MN, Broadleaf Books.

Grayling, A. C. (2007) *Against All Gods: Six Polemics on Religion and an Essay on Kindness*, London, Oberon Books.

Hinnells, J. R. (ed.) (2005) *The Routledge Companion to the Study of Religion*, London, Routledge.

Holloway, M. and Moss, B. (2010) *Spirituality and Social Work*, Basingstoke, Palgrave Macmillan.

Nolan, S. and Holloway, M. (2014) *A-Z of Spirituality*, Basingstoke, Palgrave Macmillan.

Parsons, W. B. (ed.) (2018) *Being Spiritual but Not Religious: Past, Present, Future(s)*, London, Routledge.

Seabright, P. (2024) *The Divine Economy: How Religions Compete for Wealth, Power, and People*, Princeton, NJ, Princeton University Press.

Sheldrake, P. (2014) *Spirituality: A Guide for the Perplexed*, London, Bloomsbury.

Stephens, M. (2014) *Imagine There's No Heaven: How Atheism Helped Create the Modern World*, Basingstoke, Palgrave Macmillan.

References

Ali, K. (2016) *Sexual Ethics and Islam: Feminist Reflections on Qur'an, Hadith, and Jurisprudence*, 2nd edn, Oxford, Oneworld Publications.

Armstrong, K. (1993) *A History of God*, London, Vintage.

Armstrong, K. (2010) *The Case for God: What Religion Really Means*, London, Vintage Books.

Barnes, C. and Mercer, G. (2010) *Exploring Disability*, 2nd edn, Cambridge, Polity.

Bauman, Z. (2005) *Work, Consumerism and the New Poor*, Maidenhead, Open University Press.

Biestek, F. (1957) *The Casework Relationship*, Chicago, Chicago University Press.

Bevan, S. and Cooper, C. L. (2022) *The Healthy Workforce: Enhancing Wellbeing and Productivity in the Workers of the Future*, Bingley, Emerald Publishing.

Bourdieu, P. (2021) *Forms of Capital: General Sociology, Volume 3: Lectures at the Collège de France 1983-84*, Cambridge, Polity.

Bist, D., Shuttleworth, M., Smith, L., Smith, P. and Walker-Gleaves, C. (2024) 'Music and Spirituality: An Auto-ethnographic Study of How Five Individuals Used Music to Enrich their Soul', *Religions*, 15(7), 858. https://doi.org/10.3390/rel15070858

Bowie, F. (2006) *The Anthropology of Religion: An Introduction*, 2nd edn, Oxford, Blackwell.

Bowpitt, G. (1998) 'Evangelical Christianity, Secular Humanism, and the Genesis of British Social Work', *British Journal of Social Work*, 28, pp. 675–93.

Brandon, D. (2000) *Tao of Survival: Spirituality in Social Care and Counselling*, Birmingham, Venture Press.

Canda, E. R, Furman, L. D. and Canda, H-J. (2020) *Spiritual Diversity in Social Work Practice: The Heart of Helping*, 3rd edn, Oxford, Oxford University Press.

Channer, Y. (1998) 'Understanding and Managing Conflict in the Learning Process: Christians Coming Out', in Cree and McCaulay (1998).

Chavez, J., Cullan, J. and Adaliaan, H. (2024) 'Message Patterns through Discourse Analysis on the Concept of Apology and Forgiveness during Ramadan among College Students Practicing Islam', *Environment and Social Psychology*, 9(3), https://doi.org/10.54517/esp.v913.2043

Cheese, P. (2021) *The New World of Work: Shaping A Future that Helps People, Organizations and Our Societies to Thrive*, London, Kogan Page.

Clark, J. (2012) 'Reconciliation via Truth? A Study of South Africa's TRC', *Journal of Human Rights*, 11(2), pp. 189–209.

Cleary, T. (2003) *The Taoist Classics: The Collected Translations of Thomas Cleary, Volume 2*, Boston, MA, Shambhala.

Cox, G. R. and Thompson, N. (2020) 'Making Sense of Spirituality', in Thompson and Cox (2020).

Cree, V. and McCaulay, C. (eds) (1998) *Transfer of Learning in Professional and Vocational Education*, London, Routledge.

Cunningham, M. (2012) *Integrating Spirituality in Clinical Social Work Practice: Walking the Labyrinth*, Boston, Pearson.

The Dalai Lama (2011) *Beyond Religion: Ethics for a Whole World*, London, Rider.

Davies, D. J. (2014) 'Religion', in Brennan, M. (ed) (2014) *The A-Z of Death and Dying: Social, Medical and Cultural Aspects*, Santa Barbara, CA, Greenwood.

Dobson, M. S. and Wilson, S. B. (2008) *Goal Setting: How to Create an Action Plan and Achieve Your Goals*, New York, Amacom.

Doka, K. and Morgan, J. D. (eds) (1993) *Death and Spirituality*, Amityville, NY, Baywood.

Durkheim, E. (1912) *The Elementary Forms of the Religious Life*, London, George, Alien & Unwin.

Eliot, T. S. (1944) *Four Quartets*, London, Faber and Faber.

Ellis, M. (2000) *Revolutionary Forgiveness: Essays on Judaism, Christianity and the Future of Religious Life*, Waco, TX, Baylor University Press.

Etzioni, A. (1995) *The Spirit of Community: Rights, Responsibilities and the Communitarian Agenda*, London, Fontana.

Foley, M. (2011) *The Age of Absurdity: Why Modern Life Makes it Hard to be Happy*, London, Simon & Schuster.

Foster, C. (2009) *The Selfless Gene: Living with God and Darwin*, London, Hodder and Stoughton.

Foucault, M. (1988) *Politics, Philosophy, Culture: Interviews and Other Writings 1977–1984*, New York, Routledge.

Frankl, V. E. (2000) *Man's Search for Meaning*, New York, Basic Books.

Franz, T. et al. (2001) 'Positive Outcomes of Losing a Loved One', in Neimeyer (2001).

Gardner, H. (2006) *Multiple Intelligences: New Horizons in Theory and Practice*, New York, Basic Books.

Garvin, C. (ed.) (1998) 'Special Issue: Forgiveness', *Reflections. Narratives of Professional Helping* 4(4).

Gibran, K. (ed.) (1980; originally published 1926) *The Prophet*, London, Pan Books.

Gibson, J. (2006) 'Overcoming Apartheid: Can Truth Reconcile a Divided Nation?' The *Annals of the Academy of Political and Social Science*, 603(1), pp. 82–110.

Gordon, H. (2000) 'Guilt: Why is it Such a Burden?', *Bishop John Robinson Fellowship Newsletter*, 9, pp. 4–6.

Gorelik, G. (2016) 'The Evolution of Transcendence', *Evolutionary Psychological Science*, 2(4) pp. 287–307.

Grayling, A. C. (2004) *The Mystery of Things*, London, Weidenfeld & Nicholson.

Green, L. (2010) *Understanding the Life Course: Sociological and Psychological Perspectives*, Cambridge, Polity.

Gutierrez, G. (2001) *Theology of Liberation*, London, SCM Press.

Hägglund, M. (2019) *This Life: Why Mortality Makes Us Free*, London, Profile Books.

Haidt, J. (2013) *The Righteous Mind: Why Good People Are Divided by Politics and Religion*, New York, Pantheon Books.

Haidt, J. (2024) *The Anxious Generation: How the Great Rewiring of Childhood Is Causing the Epidemic of Mental Illness*, London, Penguin.

Hamilton, M. (1995) *The Sociology of Religion: Theoretical and Comparative Perspectives*, 2nd edn, London, Routledge.

Hamm, S., Zimmer, Z. and Ofstedal, M. (2024) 'Linking Multi-dimensional Religiosity in Childhood and Later Adulthood: Implications for Later Life Health', *Research on Aging*, 47(2), pp. 91–102.

Harari, Y. N. (2015) *Homo Deus: A Brief History of Tomorrow*, London, Vintage.

Hari, J. (2018) *Lost Connections: Uncovering the Real Causes of Depression – and the Unexpected Solutions*, London, Bloomsbury.

Hari, J. (2022) *Stolen Focus: Why You Can't Pay Attention*, London, Bloomsbury.

Harrison, P. (ed.) (2010) *The Cambridge Companion to Science and Religion*, Cambridge, Cambridge University Press.

Henery, N. (2003) 'The Reality of Visions: Contemporary Theories of Spirituality in Social Work', *British Journal of Social Work*, 33(8), pp. 1105–1113.

Hitchens, C. (2007) *God Is Not Great: How Religion Poisons Everything*, London, Atlantic Books.

Hodge, D. R. (2003) *Spiritual Assessment: Handbook for Helping Professionals*, Botsford, CT, North American Association of Christians in Social Work.

Hodge, D. R., Boynton, H. M., Vis, J., Graham, J. R., Coholic, D. and Canda, E. R. (2024) 'Spirituality in Social Work Practice: Myth or Essential Component of Ethical and Effective Service Provision?', *Journal of Social Work*, 25(2). https://doi.org/10.1177/14680173241279028

Holloway, R. (2005) *Looking in the Distance: The Human Search for Meaning*, Edinburgh, Canongate.

Holloway, M. and Moss, B. (2010) *Spirituality and Social Work*, Basingstoke, Palgrave Macmillan.

Hunt, S. (2002) *Religion in Western Society*, Basingstoke, Palgrave Macmillan.

Illouz, E. (2012) *Why Love Hurts: A Sociological Explanation*, Cambridge, Polity.

Jaeggi, R. (2016) *Alienation*, New York, Columbia University Press.

Jaffe, S. (2021) *Work Won't Love You Back: How Devotion to Our Jobs Keeps Us Exploited, Exhausted and Alone*, London, Hurst & Co.

James, A., Kaur-Colbert, S. Hannah, H., Hicks, N. and Robinson, V. (2020) 'Enacting Truth and Reconciliation through Community-University Partnerships', *Engage!* 1(3), pp. 18–31. https://doi.org/10.18060/24047

Kaasa, A. (2013) 'Religion and Social Capital: Evidence from European Countries', *International Review of Sociology*, 23(3), pp. 578–596.

Kant, I. (1952) *The Critique of Judgement* (originally published in 1790), Oxford, Oxford University Press.

Kübler-Ross, E. (1969) *On Death and Dying*, New York, Macmillan.

Kneale, M. (2013) *An Atheist's History of Belief: Understanding Our Most Extraordinary Invention*, London, Bodley Head.

Lloyd [Holloway], M. (1996) 'Philosophy and Religion in the Face of Death and Bereavement', *Journal of Religion and Health*, 35(4), pp. 295–310.

Lloyd [Holloway], M. (1997) 'Dying and Bereavement, Spirituality and Social Work in a Market Economy of Welfare', *British Journal of Social Work*, 27(2), pp. 175–190.

Loue, S. (2017) *Handbook of Religion and Spirituality in Social Work Practice and Research*, New York, Springer.

Loy, D. (2010). *Imagination as Liberation: Lucid Dreams, Buddhism, and the Market*. Albany, NY, SUNY Press.

Mannheim, K. (1936) *Ideology and Utopia: An Introduction to the Sociology of Knowledge*, New York, Harcourt, Brace and World.

McGrath, A. (2015) *Inventing the Universe*, London, Hodder and Stoughton.

Merleau-Ponty, M. (2013) *Phenomenology of Perception*, London, Routledge.

Micklethwait, J. and Wooldridge, A. (2009) *God Is Back: How the Global Rise of Faith Is Changing the World*, London, Penguin.

Mochon, D., Norton, M. I. and Ariely, D. (2011) 'Who Benefits from Religion?', *Social Indicator Research*, 101, pp. 1–15.

Morgan, J. D. (1983) 'The Existential Quest for Meaning', in Doka, K. J. and Morgan, J. D. (eds) *Death and Spirituality*, Amityville, NY, Baywood.

Morgan, J. D. (1993) 'The Existential Quest for Meaning', in Doka and Morgan (1993).

Moss, B. (2002) 'Spirituality: A Personal Perspective', in Thompson (2002).

Moss, B. (2020) 'Spirituality: A Personal Perspective', in Thompson and Cox (2020).

Neimeyer, R. (ed.) (2001) *Meaning Reconstruction and the Experience of Loss*, Washington, DC, American Psychological Association.

Neimeyer, R. and Anderson, A. (2002) 'Meaning Reconstruction Theory', in Thompson (2002).

Neuberger, J. (2019) *Anyisemitism: What It Is. What It Isn't. Why It Matters*, London, Weidenfeld & Nicolson.

Nietzsche, F. (1998) *Thus Spake Zarathustra*, Ware, Wordsworth Editions.

Nolan, S. and Holloway, M. (2014) *A-Z of Spirituality*, Basingstoke, Palgrave Macmillan.

Norman, R. (2004) 'Nature, Science, and the Sacred', in Rogers (2004).

Onfray, M. (2011) *Atheist Manifesto: The Case against Christianity, Judaism, and Islam*, New York, Arcade.

Patel, N., Naik, D. and Humphries, B. (eds) (1997) *Visions of Reality: Religion and Ethnicity in Social Work*, London, Central Council for Education and Training in Social Work.

Patel, N., Naik, D. and Humphries, B. (1998) *Visions of Reality: Religion and Ethnicity in Social Work*, London, Central Council for Education and Training in Social Work.

Perez, C. C. (2019) *Invisible Women: Exposing Data Bias in a World Designed for Men*, London, Chatto & Windus.

Pew Research Center (2025) *Religious Switching in 36 Countries: Many Leave Their Childhood Religions*, https://www.pewresearch.org/religion/2025/03/26/around-the-world-many-people-are-leaving-their-childhood-religions/.

Powell, A. (2003) *Psychiatry and Spirituality: The Forgotten Dimension*, Brighton, Pavilion/NIMHE.

Quiller Couch, A. (1923) 'Armistice Day Anniversary Sermon', Cambridge, November.

Robertson, R. (1970) *The Sociological Interpretation of Religion*, Oxford, Blackwell.

Rogers, B. (ed.) (2004) *Is Nothing Sacred?* London, Routledge.

Roussopoulos, D. (ed.) (2008) *Faith in Faithlessness: An Anthology of Atheism*, London, Black Rose Books.

Rubin. R. (2025) *The Creative Act: A Way of Being*, Edinburgh, Canongate.

Rutter, M. (1999) 'Resilience Concepts and Findings: Implications for Family Therapy', *Journal of Family Therapy*, 21, pp. 119–44.

Rutter, M. (2000) 'Resilience Re-considered: Conceptual Considerations, Empirical Findings and Policy Implications', in Shankoff and Meisels (2000).

Ryan, J. S. and Burchell, M. J. (2023) *Make Work Healthy: Create a Sustainable Organization with High-performing Employees*, Hoboken, NJ, John Wiley & Sons.

Saks, A. M. and Gruman, J. A. (2021) *Advanced Introduction to Employee Engagement*, Cheltenham, Edward Elgar.

Sartre, J-P. (1989) *No Exit and Three Other Plays*, New York, Vintage.

Schumacher, E. F. (1973) *Small Is Beautiful: Economics as if People Mattered*, London, Blond & Briggs.

Scraton, P. (2016) *Hillsborough: The Truth*, 2nd edn, London, Transworld Publishing.

Shabi, R. (2024) *Off White: The Truth about Antisemitism*, London, Oneworld.

Shankoff, J. P. and Meisels, S. J. (eds) (2000) *Handbook of Early Childhood Interventions*, Cambridge, Cambridge University Press.

Smith, C. (1998) *American Evangelicalism: Embattled and Thriving, Chicago*, University of Chicago Press.

Starlyte, D. (2024) 'The Realization of Emptiness in Zen Satori: A Narrative View', in Jones, P (ed.) (2025) *Happiness and the Psychology of Enlightenment - An Investigation into Methods and Results*, London, IntechOpen.

Stroebe, M. and Schut, H. (1999) 'The Dual Process Model of Coping with Bereavement: Rationale and Description', *Death Studies*, 23(3), pp. 197–224.

Swinton, J. (2001) *Spirituality and Mental Health Care: Rediscovering a 'Forgotten' Dimension*, London, Jessica Kingsley Publishers.

Tallis, R. (2018) *Logos: The Mystery of How We Make Sense of the World*, Newcastle upon Tyne, Agenda Publishing.

Tanyi, R. (2002) 'Towards Clarification of the Meaning of Spirituality', *Journal of Advanced Nursing*, 39(5), pp. 500–09.

Thakur, S. (1996) *Religion and Social Justice*, Basingstoke, Macmillan.

Thompson, N. (ed.) (2002) *Loss and Grief: A Guide for Human Services Practitioners*, Basingstoke, Palgrave Macmillan.

Thompson, N. (2007) 'Spirituality: An Existentialist Perspective', *Illness, Crisis & Loss*, 15(2), pp. 125–36.

Thompson, N. (2017) *Theorizing Practice*, 2nd edn, London, Bloomsbury.

Thompson, N. (2018a) *Applied Sociology*, New York, Routledge.

Thompson, N. (2018b) *Promoting Equality: Working with Diversity and Difference*, 5th edn, London, Bloomsbury.

Thompson, N. (2019a) *Lessons for Living: 101 Top Tips for Optimal Well-being at Work and Beyond*, Wrexham, Avenue Media Solutions.

Thompson, N. (2019b) *Mental Health and Well-being: Alternatives to the Medical Model*, New York, Routledge.

Thompson, N. (2021a) *Anti-Discriminatory Practice: Equality, Diversity and Social Justice*, 7th edn, London, Bloomsbury.

Thompson, N. (2021b) *Anti-Racism for Beginners*, Wrexham, Avenue Media Solutions.

Thompson, N. (2022) *The Loss and Grief Practice Manual*, Wrexham, Avenue Media Solutions.

Thompson, N. (2024a) *The Learning from Practice Manual*, 2nd edn, London, Jessica Kingsley Publishers.

Thompson, N. (2024b) *Managing Stress*, 2nd edn, London, Routledge.

Thompson, N. (2025a) *Authentic Leadership Revisited*, 2nd edn, Cheltenham, Edward Elgar.

Thompson, N. (2025b) *Crisis Intervention*, 3rd edn, London, Routledge.

Thompson, N. (2025c) *Effective Problem Solving*, 2nd edn, London, Routledge.

Thompson, N. and Cox, G. R. (eds) (2020) *Promoting Resilience: Responding to Adversity, Vulnerability and Loss*, New York, Routledge.

Thompson, N. and Cox, G. R. (2025) *Age and Dignity: Anti-ageist Theory and Practice*, Cheltenham, Edward Elgar.

Thompson, N. and McGowan, J. (2024) *How to Survive in Social Work*, 2nd edn, London, Jessica Kingsley Publishers.

Thompson, N. and Moss, B. (2026) *Values-Based Practice*, 2nd edn, London, Routledge.

Thompson, S. (2025) *The Care of Older People*, 2nd edn, London, Routledge.

Tolle, E. (1999) *The Power of Now: A Guide to Spiritual Enlightenment*, Jackson, FL, New World Library.

Tolle, E. (2005) *A New Earth: Awakening to Your Life's Purpose*, New York, Penguin.

Vaughan, F. (2002) 'What is Spiritual Intelligence?', *Journal of Humanistic Psychology*, 42(2), pp. 16–33.

Warsi, S. (2024) *Muslims Don't Matter*, London, The Bridge Street Press.

Williams, B. cited in Pettit, P. and Schwieso, J. (eds) (1995) *Aspects of the History of British Social Work*, Thesis: Faculty of Education and Community Studies, University of Reading.

Zohar, D. and Marshall, I. (2000) *Connecting with Our Spiritual Intelligence*, London, Bloomsbury.

For Product Safety Concerns and Information please contact our EU
representative GPSR@taylorandfrancis.com
Taylor & Francis Verlag GmbH, Kaufingerstraße 24, 80331 München, Germany

www.ingramcontent.com/pod-product-compliance
Lightning Source LLC
Chambersburg PA
CBHW052007270326
41929CB00015B/2821

9 781041 160120